LENA

D0168411

MARGARET JENSEN

HARVEST HOUSE PUBLISHERS
Eugene, Oregon 97402

Except for some paraphrasing by the author, Scripture quotations are taken from the King James Version of the Bible.

LENA

Copyright © 1985 Margaret T. Jensen
Published by Harvest House Publishers
Eugene, Oregon 97402

Cataloging-in-Publication Data

Jensen, Margaret T. (Margaret Tweten), 1916-
    Lena / Margaret Jensen.
        p. cm.
    Originally published: San Bernardino, CA: Here's Life Publishers,
©1985.
      ISBN 1-56507-508-0
      1. Jensen, Margaret T. (Margaret Tweten), 1916– . 2. Rogers, Lena.
3. Christian biography—United States. I. Title.
BR1725.J43A3 1996   96-3674
209'.2'273—dc20   CIP

Printed in the United States of America.

96 97 98 99 00 01 02 /BC/ 10 9 8 7 6 5 4 3 2 1

To Lena Rogers Leach, maid of honor,
who brought the joy of laughter and commonsense
wisdom into everyday living.

On March 19, 1996, Lena went home to
be with the Lord she loved.
Her faith has now been made sight.

Contents

In loving memory of my husband, Harold,
whose faithful encouragement, in addition to
transferring my penned scrawl to the typewriter,
made working together as one a joy.
He went Home October 31, 1991.

I'm still writing!

A special thank-you . . .

To Greensboro College,
Greensboro, North Carolina, for the beautiful
setting for a special infirmary.

To Gordon College, Wenham, Massachusetts,
for the prayers and concern for the "rebels"
who later returned to
"go into all the world" with honor.

To the new friends at Harvest House Publishers,
who returned this enduring book
to the marketplace.

To Linda Britton,
who puts my handwritten words
into the computer.
Harold must chuckle in heaven when he
sees her praying for the gift of interpretation.

Thanks to family and friends
who prayed without ceasing until the
believing became the seeing (2 Corinthians 2:14).

1

The Approaching Footsteps

The morning breeze blew softly over the lake while the sun's rays slipped between the trees to etch a path for a new day.

My car moved slowly as I breathed in the North Carolina morning. Starmount Drive curved around the lake before it eased into Market Street. The traffic increased as I neared Greensboro College, a Methodist school, formerly for women only.

Greensboro College sat on a knoll, overlooking spacious lawns, fragrant magnolia trees, and azalea gardens. Towering oaks and pines stood like sentinels, guarding the memories of yesterday.

I guided my car into the "Reserved for Nurse" parking space, and reached for the key to unlock the door to the college infirmary.

It was an old building with spacious rooms, high ceilings, and tall windows. My office overlooked the well-worn path to the snack shop.

It was from this window that I would hear the rumblings of the late sixties, as students congregated to exchange their views on life in general, and their own ideas in particular. Even on this, my first day, I sensed an undercurrent of uneasiness. It seemed that young people were like boats loosed from their moorings, becoming slaves to the tide of our times.

Even our own son, Ralph.

A gnawing fear for our youngest gripped me. He had just enrolled as a freshman at Gordon College, Wenham, Massachusetts, but might he now be loosening the tacklings on his boat? Could that relentless tide be pulling him out to sea? I wondered—then dismissed the idea as absurd. His older sister, Janice, and brother, Dan, were well-adjusted young people. Ralph, too, would find his place.

I missed my tall lean son, whose mischievous blue eyes saw adventure in every situation.

It would pass, I mused—Gordon was a fine Christian college and my handsome rebel now was far away from his old friends and old haunts. I breathed a sigh of relief and turned to the task at hand—managing a college infirmary.

At 6:30 A.M. it was quiet in the empty building, so I went into the large kitchen, past the steam radiators, and into a pantry where I found an obviously much-used coffeepot. Upstairs, warm September breezes blew through the open windows, airing lumpy mattresses which had been draped over high metal hospital beds. I made a mental note that eighteen students could be admitted, and extra cots put up for emergencies.

The infirmary was clean, even freshly painted.

The old-fashioned beds reminded me of nurses' training days, forty years ago, when I had to scrub everything in sight for the first three months. I could see our director of nurses now, her red hair piled high on her head, and a starched cap perched precariously on the top. Miss Rosie would fold her arms across her ample bosom and announce to the terrified probationers, "Discipline, my girls. Yes. Discipline is the first rule." With a meaningful warning look she marched down the hall, her starched, ankle-length uniform crackling with stiffness. A wide belt was fastened below her waist.

I laughed to myself as I remembered a time Hertha, my roommate, and I had been practicing corners in bed making. Out of boredom my dramatic roommate recited passages from an old book in which Anthony whispered sweet nothings into Cleopatra's shell-pink ear. With an awarding performance Hertha acted out the part, that is, until Miss Rosie walked in to check the corners. We never found out what Anthony whispered to Cleopatra.

With all those beds to make, I couldn't help but think of Miss Rosie who kept me in fear of being sent home or of being duly reported to my father, then pastor of the First Norwegian Baptist Church in Chicago. However, as is often the case, the thing I feared had not come to pass. In 1937 I graduated from the Norwegian American Hospital Training School in Chicago with my R.N. degree. Papa proudly pronounced the benediction.

Walking around the old building, so reminiscent of the past, I sensed the years since then flowing together. The events moved as though on a screen: assistant director of nurses, teaching in the school of practical nursing, private duty, office nurse, and now I was a college infirmary nurse. First and last I was Harold's wife, and the mother of three children now gone from the nest. Perhaps that is why these students seemed like my own children. I wondered how this river would flow.

My thoughts were brought back to the reality of the present when I heard Dean Locke's booming voice, "Good morning, Florence Nightingale! You should be so lucky as to get the best maid on campus for infirmary housekeeper." With a sweeping bow he announced, "Meet Lena Rogers, the queen of the pound cakes." In a moment he was gone, racing across the campus as he waved to returning students, then disappearing behind the stone walls of the administration building.

I turned to face smiling eyes and clasped two black hands in a welcoming gesture. Laughingly Lena said, "I best be cooking that dean a pound cake," but her knowing eyes looked deeply into mine. Her face was a velvet darkness, and I found myself thinking, *a symphony in black.*

"Nurse Jensen, looks like me and you got us a job. Lord have mercy, I never had no baby, and now I gets a college full of young'uns. You take care of the pills and I take care of the pots. I best tend to the kitchen, then we can have a cup of tea." Her joyous singing soon filled the empty building.

Later, we sat quietly together at the kitchen table. I read from my worn Bible: "In all thy ways acknowledge Him, and He shall direct thy paths."[1]

In my heart I knew that my introduction to Lena in September, 1968, at Greensboro College, Greensboro, North Carolina, was an introduction to a challenging friendship.

2

Calling Out Your Name

The infirmary door banged open and I heard a frantic, "Where's Lena?"

"Lord have mercy, child, in the kitchen. Where else? Don't go bangin' no doors in my house, boy." Lena's laughing eyes and bear hug countered her law-and-order command.

"Lena, I'm starved. I overslept and can't make the dining room. Got any toast and coffee?"

Jim eased his six-foot frame into a chair, and between bites and gulps confessed his fears about girls, exams—and life.

"While you're swallowing your food whole I'll sing you a song and then come back when me and you can talk. Every day, son, I stands by this window and looks to that tree, and I says, 'Big tree, you been there in long years gone. You been in the winter and the storm, the spring and the summer. You changes colors, but you still stand. You done watched my children coming and going. You're there when the children go home for the summer and you still standing when they comes back.'

"You know something, Jim? Me and that tree is the same. We both gets life from God. The Bible says that this black Lena is like a tree planted by the rivers of water and the leaf shall not wither and what Lena does shall prosper. My roots are in Jesus—that's my roots—and I drink of the river of life, and when that tree is gone, long gone, this Lena still stands forever with the Lord. All that learning you getting, boy, who is telling you that?"

Lost in her own thoughts, Lena sang softly, "Without Him I would be nothing...."

"You best go to your class, and I'll be here watching and calling out your name."

From my window I heard Jim's whistle as he raced across the campus to get to his first class. From the kitchen came Lena's plaintive cry, "Oh, Lord, hear Your child. I'm calling out Jim's name. Bless him, Lord, and all my children. Bless this here infirmary and all those folks with so much learning from books, but let them get learning from You, Lord. This is Lena, Lord, I come most all the time, so You knows Your black child real good. I knows You too and You don't never fail Your Lena. Thank You."

Within moments Lena was tapping her feet and patting her hands while she sang, "Power in the Blood." She was having her own church time with the Lord.

I stopped my paperwork to open my Bible, where I read, "But his delight is in the law of the Lord; and in His law doth he mediate day and night."[1] Another psalm said, "Day unto day uttereth speech, and night unto night sheweth knowledge."[2] I thought about the days and nights of our lives, the joys and sorrows, the agonies and the ecstasies—all part of that river of life. We learn from God through it all. The day, a time of working for Him, and the night, a time to rest in Him. When we see clearly, we act, when it is dark, we trust. In trusting comes the knowing that God works all things together for good.

My "church time" was interrupted with Lena's, "Here they comes, Nurse Jensen. The throats, the cramps, the allergies, the bad nerves, the wounded, and the homesick with the vomiting or the diarrhea. Didn't know young folks had so many ailments." She rolled her eyes heavenward with a prayer, "Lord, help them when they gets old."

When the doctor arrived for the daily office hour, Lena pulled him aside, "You looks plumb tuckered out like you been drove hard and put up wet. Here, eat this bowl of soup and cheese sandwich. No one out there dying, mostly wants attention, first time away from home."

With a sigh he sat down and the tension eased out of his face. It had been a rough morning and he faced his own office of waiting patients.

Lena quietly pointed to her tree, "That tree gonna be here when me and you is plumb gone; but, then again, we will be living when that tree is gone."

Oblivious to anyone around her she sang—

> When we've been there ten thousand years,
> Bright shining as the sun,
> We've no less days to sing God's praise,
> Than when we first begun.

When sick call was ended, the doctor's orders were given: X-rays for possible fractures, chest films, throat cultures, special prescriptions.

All day the students came—before, between, and after classes. Many stopped by the kitchen for a brief visit. Each one received a pat and a hug, and lingered to hear a song or a Lena lecture.

Lena's eyes followed the students as they walked across the campus. The wind carried her promise, "I'll be calling out your name."

One day, later in the fall, Lena said to me, "Nurse Jensen, don't forget the medicine man is coming." She went to put the toast in the oven while I retreated to my office to complete the medical supply list before the pharmaceutical salesman arrived.

Students were passing under my window, and before long I overheard one of them say, "Go on in and see the nurse. Maybe she'll help you."

"Why should she help me? I'm not a student anymore. Nothing but bad luck for me, and now I'm sick and have no money."

"Go on, and see her anyhow. She never turns anyone away. I don't know why, but I just know she loves us."

I continued writing at my desk, but stopped when I heard a step outside the office. Looking up I saw a long-haired young man with a lean, gaunt look, wearing faded blue jeans and sandals. He complained of nausea, headache, dizziness and weakness. He was jittery and fumbling in his pockets.

About that time Lena came around the corner and took one look at the hollow eyes.

"Tells you what, boy, while nurse gets you some medicine, you best come in the kitchen where Lena keeps her medicine—oven toast, scrambled eggs, and coffee."

He followed Lena quietly and watched her stir the eggs. "Life do get scrambled around like these eggs—but we comes out pretty good when God gets us out of the frying pan." She laughed and poured him coffee.

He ate without looking up, but finally, when the empty eyes looked into Lena's knowing eyes, the words tumbled out. "I had no place to go. My folks divorced. My wife couldn't find a job, and we got on drugs. I couldn't keep up my classes and now I'm out. My old roommate told me to come here."

"Can't do nothing until you get your stomach straightened out child. All that smoking, drinking, dope stuff got your insides all twisted around. You needs some good oatmeal in that stomach. You come back in the morning and me and you can talk. Can't talk on a empty stomach nohow—head don't work too good. I tells you what—you best bring your wife today for a grilled cheese for lunch. Some things don't take to waiting. God has a way and man has his way that he thinks is right. Jesus says, 'I am the way.'³ We all has to choose sometime. But time enough for choosing. Now is time for eating."

When the young man left he promised to return with his wife at noon.

Within a short time the door opened again, and a handsome young man introduced himself as the new pharmaceutical representative. Since I had several students to see first, he accepted Lena's offer of coffee. Within moments I heard conversation flowing between Lena and this "medicine man."

When I finished I joined them with my list, and went over the needed supplies.

Before he left, Lena said quietly, "We needs to pray for this family. God going to give this man a baby."

The story unfolded that he and his wife were in the process of adoption. It seemed they had waited for years for a child, and now it was working out. There would soon be a baby available.

"The Bible says, 'Train up a child in the way he should go,' and I asks you what way you be thinking about training that baby God be giving you?" Lena looked into the face of the expectant father.

"I don't know," he faltered, "never thought much about it."

"Now is a good time," continued Lena, "for you, the papa, to be getting the house in order, before God gives you that baby. Jesus said, 'I am the way.' First, you get in the right way, then the mama, and then you both teach the baby the right way. Sing, 'Jesus loves me' and that baby will grow up the right way."

Lena sang softly, rocking the imaginary baby in her arms.

> Jesus loves me this I know
> For the Bible tells me so.

The kitchen was quiet. Lena added softly, "What is there any greater to know? Jesus right here in my kitchen, and wants to take you by the hand and show you the right way." She sang—

> Precious Lord, take my hand
> Lead me on, let me stand.

With head bowed she prayed, "We just poor little lambs that don't know nothing, so take us by the hand and make us something. Help this papa and mama to know You and give them this baby they been waiting for. Thank You, Jesus."

Then he was gone, with the list of medical supplies in hand. When he waved from the car, Lena waved back from her post at the window, and I heard her calling out his name.

Lena continued her work, gathering up laundry, changing beds. There were food supplies to order, kitchen and bathrooms to clean, floors to mop and furniture to dust. The phone rang incessantly and the door opened to students, salesmen, laundry men, delivery boys and friends who stopped by to say hello.

"Faith and works goes together," was Lena's theme. She kept the Bible open on the kitchen table and prayed and sang as she worked.

Before I could finish my morning office work I heard Lena—"Time for lunch, nurse, got some good cottage cheese and pineapple and a crust of bread." The crust of bread was cheese melted on oven toast, with a cup of Lena tea. No one knew exactly what Lena had in her tea, but I was sure she used fruit juice and spices. When the students asked about the delicious tea she answered, "Prayer, children, prayer, I just puts praising and praying in the tea. Cures most everything."

We agreed.

For a few moments it was quiet in the kitchen and we bowed our hearts together in gratitude to God for every provision—especially for the crust of bread. We wondered if the young man, from the morning visit, would return. He seemed in such despair. "He'll come," Lena said. "The Lord will bring him back."

When our quiet lunch was completed, I returned to my desk to get ready for sick call. The doctor would be arriving soon, and so would the students.

I glanced out the window. Apparently Lena's invitation had worked, for down the driveway came the young man of the early morning with a thin girl clinging to his hand.

With a "Praise the Lord," Lena gathered the wife, dressed in a peasant dress and sandals, into her arms. "Oh, child, you come to the right place—Lena. You needs some meat on them bones, so sit down for a crust of bread." The kitchen was alive with warmth and love, and stories, songs, and laughter made two young people temporarily forget their troubles.

Before the visit came to an end, Lena had practiced her brand of psychology, "Something in the stomach first, and a good laugh to clear the head. Can't have no coonching spirits of doubt and fear clogging up the head. That Satum can't tolerate no joy."

In the meantime, one of my favorite students came in for a brief visit. Dave was a strong, handsome Christian, married to a lovely girl who worked as a dental technician to help Dave complete his senior year.

After a bear hug for Lena and me, Dave was introduced

to the young couple at the table. During the casual conversation Dave learned that the young wife was also a dental technician—unemployed. Dave perked up and invited the couple to his apartment, assuring the young woman that his own wife could give her some job tips. Turning to the husband he added, "There's always a way to finish school. Let's discuss it over supper tonight."

I watched the couple leave, hand in hand, clinging to each other against a hostile world. This time they were laughing.

Dave turned to Lena, "You pray, and God will work on the inside. My wife and I will work on the outside. You always say faith and works go together."

With a victory sign, and a "Praise the Lord," Dave was gone. I heard Lena calling out his name, "Bless him, Lord. Oh, bless him, Lord."

The day was drawing to a close. The evening nurse would be coming soon. The doctor had completed his routine sick call, and I was finishing my daily infirmary report. My student helper was waiting to bring reports to the main office. Lena was rattling her pans and I had locked up the pills. It had been quite a day, but then they were all like that—busy, with unexpected interruptions. Yet, somehow the hours of the day moved with peace and order.

Lena waved good-bye as she crossed the campus to catch her bus. I heard her singing, "One step at the time, sweet Jesus."

In my heart I heard the words, "In all thy ways acknowledge Him, and He shall direct thy paths."[4]

As my car turned around the bend of the lake toward home, I wondered about the young couple, Dave, the "medicine man" . . . and Ralph. I looked in the mailbox. Still no letter.

A week later the phone rang for Lena. "Praise the Lord," she shouted, "the medicine man done got his baby boy."

3

Sunsets Never Wait

I often forgot to turn the page of a calendar, but I couldn't turn back the clock of time.

It was November 1969, and students were preparing for Thanksgiving vacation. The kitchen was quiet. My reports were finished. No sick call today.

Looking out of the kitchen window I sensed a feeling of security in the presence of the towering oak growing in the lawn.

"What if that tree could talk, Lena? Think of all the secrets that majestic oak could tell."

Laughingly Lena answered, "Oh, but that tree do talk. It say, 'Lena, just stand where God put you, like I do. I don't fret and carry on to be a tall pine. I just be standing here, unshakable, unmovable, a shelter in the storm, and a shade in the heat.' Then I tell myself, 'Lena just be—just be abounding in the work of the Lord. Do your work as unto the Lord, for God sees the heart and is a rewarder of them who diligently seek Him.' That tree be talking, Nurse Jensen, and I talk back. I say, 'God planted you outside my kitchen, and He planted me inside this kitchen.' We just stand praising the Lord together."

I sipped my coffee. Lena put a cheese sandwich (her crust of bread) in the oven.

"I don't hear from Ralph these days, and his grades are low."

"Don't be fretting about that child, Ralph. God brought Dan home from Vietnam, and he gave Janice and Jud a knowing child. Now is the time to trust, and don't be talking so much about how good Dan be. Might put a hurting place in Ralph."

"You always get my weak spot, Lena. Harold and I almost lost Dan when he was a baby, but God spared him. He is a miracle child, and I always believed God had a special purpose for him."

"They all be special, and God has a purpose for each one. No one is better than the other. Only God knows the heart and why one can be easy to teach, and one be hard. We stand on what God says and not on what we see. God says all works for good, so why do we study so much about the bad? How do we know what seeds be sprouting in the heart? What looks so good to us might not look so good to God. What be looking so bad to us might be some chaff God let blow in the wind. Peter and Paul didn't look too good at one time, but there be a heap of turning around for good when God got hold of them."

I tried to put aside the nagging fear about Ralph, and allow the joy of the arrival of our first grandchild to fill my thoughts. Heather Dawne Carlberg.

I turned the pages of memory to when our Janice was born, just as dawn came over the skyscrapers of Chicago. She was our spring and summer rolled into one; a joy from the very first day.

"In those early years I began praying for a prince for our little princess. I prayed that, as we taught Janice to love the

Lord, God was preparing a little boy to love God—and our Janice. I can't believe that our baby girl is a mother, Lena."

"God says it's not good for man to be alone. Two people loving God together be better than one. Who knows, maybe there will be someone for me someday. Now, I stay in God's plan to me, and that means to obey one step at the time. I not be forgetting that without Him I would be nothing."

As Lena looked out toward her oak tree, a shadow crossed her face.

"One time, long ago, some white folks treat me like I be nothing. When they were gone I crawled under the dining room table and cried. I felt so scroonched up like a nothing ball. Then God put a knowing in my heart. 'Lena, you belong to me. You are a child of the King.' That knowing never left me."

"Oh, Lena, that 'scroonched-up nothing ball' feeling comes to all of us." I picked up the worn Bible and read John 17:9, 10: "I pray . . . for them which thou has given me; for they are thine. And all mine are thine, and thine are mine; and I am glorified in them."

We sensed God's presence with a "knowing" that we belonged to our heavenly Father.

With a "thank You, Jesus," Lena poured another cup of coffee. This time she said, "Sit down, Jesus, and have a cup of coffee with us. I can see You right here in my kitchen. The eye of faith sees better than the natural eye."

I agreed!

"Now tell me about the boy prince you prayed for," Lena laughed. "Jesus likes to hear us talking about our blessing. The angels must be shaking their heads at what doubting fools we be."

"Oh, Lena, God must love you special!" I continued, "Jan met Jud at Wheaton College in Illinois, where they were students together, class officers, and the prince and princess in the special college play. They even sang the Hawaiian wedding song together and were called the campus sweethearts.

"Harold and I loved Jud when we first met him, and I knew this tall handsome young man, with the deep blue eyes, had indeed been kept by the power of God. His quiet disciplined life will make him a great college administrator."

"Good thing he got Janice to sparkle up his life since he be so smart and dignified like. Best part though, he got the wisdom of God before the book learning. Put the two together and you have a man who can change the world. Trouble is most folks outgrow their common sense. God's wisdom got common sense or else how Moses be so smart? He listen to God beside all that learning he got from Pharaoh. God come first, and Moses learned more in the desert than he learned in Egypt. Trouble with folks, they don't learn where they be at. David's papa put him out to tend the sheep, like me picking cotton. I learn to be quiet, shut my mouth, think about God and His ways. That way a knowing gets in you, and God puts the knowing in there. David learned from God's creation and a few books Moses wrote. Who say thunder don't talk and lightning speak? How many times do the ocean roar and the stars sing together? Look at that sun marching across the sky like he owns the world. Nary a corner of this world not touched by the sun. He not talking? We be not hearing. How many times you think the birds try to tell us something, and we too busy rattling pots and pans to hear?"

"Professor Lena, you should be turned loose in the classroom! Wouldn't the students love that? But then, what would I do?"

"Oh, Sister Jensen, you'd find a way to organize something." Wistfully she added, "Wonder what I could have been with an education?"

"I think you would have been a wonderful teacher, Lena, but that's what you are right now, right in the kitchen. Besides, look at all your students! You could have been a great singer, but then again, here you are singing all day long."

"Better to be a depending on the Lord than to be a book-learning fool. A fool says there is no God, and some book-learnin' professors teach young folks to be fools. The fear of the Lord is the beginning of wisdom, so I best stay in the beginning. God plants His children like He plants trees, and kitchens need trees of righteousness most as much as in a classroom."

"Janice was six years old when she gave her heart to Jesus. I was also six years old when I walked down the aisle in Winnepeg, Manitoba, Canada, and asked Jesus to come into my heart. Dr. R.A. Torrey was conducting children's meetings. We never know how open children are to the gospel. Lena, when did you come to know the Lord?"

"Through my grandmother. I was born in Raeford, North Carolina. Now she was my mother's mother—my grandparents and my mother were Christians. We had to go to church even if we went barefooted, which we did sometimes. When I was about six years old I can remember my grandfather had a lot of big books. I would look at the book of Jesus and at the pictures and cry. And I had a fear inside, even when I was preachin' to the young'uns in the backyard—'If you're bad, the devil is going to get you.' As time passed on we had revival meetings, a whole week of meetings, and I asked Jesus to come into my heart. I remember that Wednesday night I was baptized in a creek. We had to walk about a mile from the church to the mill pond for baptizing—all dressed in white— and everyone sang:

> Lead me to the water,
> Lead me to the water,
> Lead me to the water,
> To be baptized.

"There was a knowing—I was God's child.

"I went to school to the sixth grade. My grandmother was a midwife and she took me along with her to gather roots for medicine. I didn't tend to no birthings, but I had a knowing about life. Years later I went to New York on a sleep-in job . . . then came back to North Carolina.

"I be always loving the Lord and working in the church. In New York I left one job in Jackson Heights to look for other work, and I had a knowing about God guiding me. Now I know it be the Holy Spirit. At night I slept with my Bible. One night the Lord gave me, 'Comfort ye, comfort ye my people,'[1] and I got a job with retarded children. I remember especially a little six-year-old who couldn't talk, but I sang songs and he learned to sing.

"My grandmother said I was a knowing child. Deep inside I get a knowing about people, but most of all I have a knowing about God. Most folks know about God, but the important thing is for God to know me. At the judgment, some people get told, 'I never knew you.' It's not the doing, but the knowing. I'd rather have God know me as His child than anything else. That be the best knowing. Jesus took me by the hand and said, 'This is Lena, Father, I died for her.' Then God look at this black child and say, 'I know Lena. She belongs to Me.' How much higher can you get?"

Oblivious to anyone around her, Lena sang quietly,

> Lead me to the water,
> Lead me to the water,
> Lead me to the water,
> To be baptized.

She was a child again . . . remembering.

I was also remembering. God has always been very real to me. I always knew I belonged to Him and that He loved me.

"I can see you preaching, Lena, because I did the same thing. I got up on a box and imitated my father. And so did Janice."

When the day's work came to an end, I found myself enfolded in Lena's parting prayer and blessing. Driving around the lake I stopped the car long enough to view the red and gold trees reflected in the lake. Honking at intruders, Dan's white and gray pet geese arched their graceful necks and moved in formation toward the shore. Behind the leaders came the white ducks, quacking for attention. They knew I would return with a bag of bread.

It was quiet by the lake and a good time for memories to follow the sun behind the trees:

> It was a long time ago. I was in DeKalb, Illinois, washing supper dishes. Quietly Danny Boy pulled on my apron strings, "Come, Mama, let's sit on the porch and watch the sun go down."
>
> "I'll come when I finish the dishes," I answered listlessly.
>
> Wistfully his blue eyes looked up at me with a knowing beyond his four years. "But Mama, don't you know that sunsets never wait?"
>
> I quickly dried my hands on my apron. Together we sat on the porch steps of the old parsonage and watched the sun go down.

Now Dan was home from Vietnam and he would enjoy more sunsets.

Soon, Harold, Dan, and I would be spending Thanksgiving with Jan and Jud and the new baby. Ralph planned his Thanksgiving in Massachusetts, but promised to be home for Christmas. In my heart I couldn't shake a nagging fear—a haunting that Lena would call "them coonching spirits."

I dismissed the weight of oppression and let my thoughts return to a happier time.

My children, like players, kept coming out on my mental stage. Inwardly I applauded, laughed, and cried.

Jan was the sparkling one, a born actress, and Dan played a good leading man, quiet, dependable, always doing the right thing. But Ralph—he was the family comedian. With dignified guests around the dining room table, Ralph would run through the house unrolling toilet tissue when he was supposed to be asleep in his crib. It was Ralph who would dump soap powder into the bathtub and then spin around to make bubbles. Once, covered in soap like a snowman, he streaked naked down the street with bubbles trailing in his path. As this show unfolded in my mind, Ralph was clearly the star.

Dan was like the anchor, steadying the boat, while Ralph was like splashing oars, in a hurry to get someplace. Janice held a brother in each hand and loved them both. Harold and I loved them all.

Reluctantly I left my rendezvous with the lake and woods. There was a quiet order in God's creation.

"The heavens declare the glory of God; and the firmament sheweth His handywork."[2] In my journal I wrote, "It is not merely glory that the heavens declare, but the glory of God, for they deliver to us such unanswerable arguments for a conscious, intelligent, planning, controlling and presiding Creator that no unprejudiced person can remain unconvinced by them.

"In the expanse above us, God flies, as it were, His starry flag to show that the King is at home."[3]

4

Winds of Winter

The frozen lake stretched between the barren trees that glistened with snow in the moonlight, and the wind blew lightly over the New England fields. The campus buildings of Gordon College, Wenham, Massachusetts, stood like fortresses against the winter coming in from Canada.

Springs kept one part of the lake from freezing solidly, but at one end, where the students could drive their cars across the ice, they started bonfires for warmth.

Ralph and Rob, Ed and David—four rebel college students—decided to slip away from the others, and they raced across the lake to the far end where they shared a forbidden bottle of brandy. They made their own rules.

Allen, Ralph's college big brother, decided to skate across the lake away from the crowd. A few minutes away would be a welcome reprieve from all the pressures. For Allen, school was soon coming to an end. In a few weeks he would graduate and begin his life's work.

With the abandonment of youth, he moved swiftly into the winter stillness.

Happy voices rang out across the winter wonderland. Boys tightened the skates of the girls, and they all pulled on warm mittens and fastened brightly knit scarves and toboggan caps. Fleece-lined jackets added color to the winter's whiteness. Songs and laughter floated across the lake and soon there was a symphony of skates in rhythm. Everyone was a part of the skaters' waltz. It was a fairyland night. It was a night no one would ever forget.

At the far end of the lake, the four rebels, warmed by the brandy, drank in the beauty of a winter moon.

Suddenly Rob saw Allen skating toward the danger zone of the lake, where hidden springs kept the ice thin. The crackling ice gave way, and a cry broke the stillness. A black hole opened and water flowed over the ice.

With the reflexes of an athlete, Rob was off like a shot, with Ralph, Ed, and Dave in pursuit. Then Rob was on the crackling ice and plunged into the inky blackness.

"I'll get Rob," screamed Ralph, "and you two get Al." Ralph reached for Rob until he struggled to the safety of a far surface. Ed plunged into the black hole to pull Allen out. "Make a chain," he screamed into the night.

By that time the cries reached the other end of the lake and the skaters moved like the wind, but black water was covering the ice. Panic-stricken, some fled; others yelled, "We're going for help."

The four formed a chain and almost succeeded in pulling Allen onto the hard surface. Ed was still in the hole trying to lift Allen, but the heavy skates, the wet clothing and the cold water were too much. Allen was pulled downstream by a fast-moving current.

The others screamed for Ed to hang on until he was finally safe on solid ice. It seemed like hours, but for those moments all time stood still.

Numb with cold and shock, the four moved their frozen legs across the ice to the dormitory. In the warm shower the clothing thawed, but their hearts were gripped by cold despair.

Their housemates' silence seemed to hang over the four rebels with quiet accusation. Later they understood it was their own silent guilt.

Warm and dry, the four found their way to the chapel. There they poured out their anguish in tears of hopelessness.

"My God, at least we tried—we tried. If we hadn't been at that end of the lake no one would have seen him. We tried, oh, God, how we tried—but where were the others? We couldn't save Al, but we tried."

In the quiet of the chapel the four wept out their bitterness and frustration, and a dark night of the soul set in over Al's departure from this life.

Into the black despair came one beam of light. "Allen was a Christian," Ralph commented quietly. "He was my college brother. He really is not dead, but home with the Lord. He was a believer. What if it had been us? Where would we be?"

"Yeah, Ralph, what about us?"

The question hung in the air like a heavy cloud, unanswered, but the seedlings of rebellion kept growing. The memory of Allen's icy hand that had slipped beyond their reach lingered like a nightmare with no waking up.

About 2 A.M. the divers found Allen's body...downstream.

At the memorial service, the light filtered through again, "I am the resurrection, and the life: he that believeth in me ...shall never die."

Into the black despair came the love and gratitude from Allen's mother: "You risked your lives to save him." They wept together as she held Ed close to her heart.

Her love cushioned the hurt, but winter stayed long in the hearts of the four rebels.

Back in Greensboro, North Carolina, I wondered why there was no mail. It was the silence of a dark winter night in my soul, too.

5

Lena's Kitchen

In confidential tones, the girls who sneaked into Lena's kitchen confided in her their fears of being ridiculed for being virgins. "I must be the only girl in school who believes in waiting for marriage," one girl cried on Lena's shoulder. "I feel like such an oddball."

"Hush, child, you know that a dozen girls already been here to say the same thing, and I expect dozens more to come when they get enough nerve to tell Lena. You want Lena to tell you what the boys tell me? Well, I won't," she laughed, "but I can say this much, there are lots a boys who want friends to talk to and go out with, but they complains that girls want to try everything: dope, liquor, and hopping into bed.

"Once you give away what God done give you to keep private and special, there's no way to go back. What for you call those parts 'private'? That's cause they do be private.

"The Bible says that we should give and it will be given unto us. You gives love, you gets love; you gives your time, you gets time; you gives friendship, you gets friendship.

Same way we are taught to give our tithes, and God blesses back.

"Now, on the other hand," Lena rolled her eyes heavenward. "Help me, Jesus. Now on the other hand, you gives hate, you gets hate. When you plant potatoes you not looking for a big ripe watermelon. No, you looks for more potatoes. You think you can plant corn and get onions? Now child, listen to your Lena. You give that 'possible' to any boy come round when God says that be your private, you gets all the possible you want, cause every boy be looking for the possible. You gets what you done give, but you lose the private.

"You think old Lena don't know nothing about 'possibles'? You think I don't know nothing about melting like hot butter when that certain big black man come to Lena all smiling like, and all the grease from the garage washed away? He be standing there on a Saturday night with clean shirt, smelling like Aqua Velva, no whiskers, and hair combed. He say, 'Lena, honey,' and, oh, child, that honey come dripping like golden sunshine. I be remembering a hard week, scrubbing floors and cooking for the white folks. All week it was 'Lena do this,' and 'Lena do that.' When I got my piece of money, the rent man was waiting and the insurance man. I had to pay the light bill and the phone. I only had enough for the bus until next week. I cooked steaks for the white folks, but I ate fat meat and hamburger. I watched folks going to town, but I couldn't go. Then, right in front of me was town coming to me. I was all clean, smelling like Avon talcum powder, ready to be cooking some greens.

"There he stands, 'Lena baby, I smells that salad, and look, honey, what I bring you, a nice big steak. How about a baked potato, a big juicy steak, and salad? Lena baby, you got skin like black velvet and I be needing you real bad.'

"My apartment look so clean and nice, but empty. Lord have mercy, but that steak would taste mighty good. I hear that, 'Lena honey,' dripping like butter and my knees get plumb weak and I get that feeling of plumb lonesomeness all over me and I be needing him like he be needing me.

"He says, so soft like, 'Lena baby, when you're hungry, you eat. When you're tired, you sleep, so if you gets this lonesome feeling for someone, and that man come to you, it be just like eating when you be hungry. Lena, honey, I be hungry for you.'

"Oh, child, you think that this Lena don't cry out to the Lord? I stay crying out to the Lord. Come Saturday night, I cry harder. I said, 'Oh, Jesus, help me.' All of a sudden them weak knees get strong, and that sweet dripping honey looked like poison. I stood tall like, and said real quiet-like, 'I be mighty busy tonight, studying my Sunday school lesson. You best be going home.'

"He left slow and sad like, but when he turned around he said, 'I'll be coming back, Lena honey.'

"That's when I close the door and lock it. I stretched out before the Lord and I cried long and hard. I be mighty lonesome for a man's loving. I ate my collards alone.

"Nowadays they talks about free love. Child, you know how much love cost? It be like you buying a steak, and somebody come and eat it up. You done paid for it, but somebody else eats it. It be like planting watermelons. You buy the seed, plow, plant, hoe, and then, about the time you ready to eat that big ripe one, somebody come along and take it.

"Now you be special . . . only one like you. God made you in His image, to grow, to love, to live, and love Him first of all. God says it is not good to be alone so he makes a boy special, to grow, to love, to live, and love God first.

"Then God says, now study to be approved, and work for the night is coming. He knows this growing up business is hard, so He says, 'Put on the whole army of God so you can fight all them coonching spirits.' There be so many coonching spirits, like doubt and unbelief, unforgiveness, resentment, and hatred.

"Oh, child, there be other coonching spirits we don't hear so much about... It's them coonching spirits of lust. That be different from love. Lust eats the steak he didn't pay for. He steals the watermelon he didn't plant. He takes the possible from one and then another and leaves nothing private. Them coonching spirits makes girls wear dresses up to the possible and the boys with pants so tight, like Lena don't know what be inside.

"I watches from my window and I see boys and girls a huggin' and a squirming. I cries out to my Jesus to help them go the right way. Jesus is the right way—the only way. That boy thinks he found a fun way and that girl thinks she doing her own way. God says, that way of rebellion to God's rules— that be sin. Sin is death.

"I hope you listens, child—not just your ears, but your heart.

"But love suffers long. It be patient to wait and kind so no sweet girl gets in trouble, and love isn't selfish, but gentle and understanding. That kind of love be strong. Come Sunday morning, my knees feel so strong and my soul feels so good I just start singing, 'Precious Lord, take my hand,' and the choir come right along and sing, 'O sweet Jesus, take my hand.'

"You know why the choir can sing right along? That be soul music. We feels the same burdens, the same lonesomeness, the same hunger, the same tired from a long week, but we feels the same Jesus taking our hand and first thing you know we got the whole church singing, 'Precious Lord take my hand,' then the joy comes and we can sing, 'Every time I feels the Spirit in my heart, I will pray.' Then we gets happy.

"The Bible says the joy of the Lord is your strength. Now I ask you child, how you be strong if you not happy? You gets your joy from the Lord, not from the world.

"You best be going child, Lena got lots of cleaning up to do, but you come back every day so we can keep the joy. Then you be strong."

The blond head rested on Lena's shoulder while the tears fell from baby blue eyes. Then, looking into Lena's black face, the girl said quietly, "Lena, I'm still private." With a burst of joy she raced across campus to the next class. I heard Lena calling out her name.

I worked quietly at my desk until Lena called me for lunch—a crust of bread (with cheese) and a cup of tea.

During our lunch I told Lena about our Thanksgiving trip to Michigan, our beautiful new granddaughter she had prayed for, and our visit to Chicago to see my sister Joyce, who was married to Howard, Harold's brother. Their three children, Judy, Paul, and Steve, and our three, Jan, Dan, and Ralph had been more like brothers and sisters than cousins. The closeness of our families was a constant reminder that God's laws and His ways are a protection from the destructive forces around us. I told her how we missed Ralph. Lena shared the "knowing" that Ralph stood in need of prayer.

Christmas holidays were drawing close and suddenly we had an idea.

"We needs joy on this campus," Lena added. "So many fine people working so hard to teach young folks, and these children be studying long hours before exams. We need a Christmas party!"

"That's it, Lena! We'll have an open house and send invitations to the various departments, and the students can help with the decorations."

For days I dragged boxes of ornaments from home and students put up decorations and trimmed a tree. We used cotton balls and made bows out of gauze.

A long table was placed in the hall and we served the cookies and cake we had baked at home. We had only one patient, and she had a ringside seat to all the activity. Judy's injured leg kept her in bed, but never did one patient have so many visitors as on the day of our open house.

The college president, Dr. Jolly, and the infirmary physician, Dr. Gilmore, balanced plates of cookies and punch as they visited with students and faculty. In the relaxed holiday atmosphere, the tensions of last-minute term papers and exams were laid aside. Vacation was nearly a reality.

Foreign students looked forward to spending the holidays with faculty members and students. Several students were coming home with me.

All too soon the happy day came to a close and the decorations were dismantled, only to be taken home and put up for our Christmas. Lena closed the kitchen door, and I locked the office. Students left for their parents' homes.

I watched Lena sing her way across campus to catch her bus, and I took the foreign students home with me.

Two of them, Moa from Singapore, and Becky from Indonesia, helped Dan put up our tree and joined in the Christmas preparations in the kitchen. Their happy giggles filled the house, and Dan's teasing made the girls feel a part of the family. They were anxious to meet Ralph who was coming home on tomorrow's flight.

Once again Harold and I were at the airport. "Seems to me there is always one of the children coming or going, but I must say I enjoy the coming the most." This time I didn't.

It wasn't just the long hair and beard, but the gaunt, hollow look.

"The thing I feared had come upon me," and what had been hints of rebellion now appeared as open defiance against the values our family held dear. Our fun-loving son had become a stranger.

Moa and Becky's gentle Oriental faces looked at me with tear-filled eyes. One time I saw them kneeling in the guest room, and I knew they were praying not only for Ralph . . . but also for me.

The joy of the Christmas season—the spice-filled kitchen, the decorations, the fragrant pine trees—brought us all together in the traditional preparations. Even Ralph was drawn into the holiday mood and I was confident that the gathering of family and friends would help to bring our son back onto the right road.

The agony and ecstasy of life I pondered long into the night. There was the ecstasy of knowing the true meaning of Christmas, and the unbearable agony of knowing our son had made a detour from the truth, the way, and the life. I finally slept, but fitfully.

It was Christmas 1969.

6

The Letter

"He's gone!" I shouted, as I reached for my coat and slippers so I could run into the icy wind after the retreating footsteps.

Within moments the house was ablaze with lights. Harold and Dan pulled trousers over their pajamas and grabbed heavy jackets and stocking caps.

"I heard the door close and footsteps down the driveway. Ralph's bed is empty, and here's a note."

December 31, 1969

Dear Mom, Dad, and Dan,

Sorry to have to leave like this, but when I have to do something for my own fulfillment, I have to try before I can do anything else.

Instead of being mad and disgusted with me, just say a big prayer for me that I make what I have planned for my new year's work. That these small dreams and whims of mine come true. That the big job finally does come along so I can take a load off your mind as well as my withered mind.

Dan, I'm sorry I couldn't have spent more time with you and done things with you. I'll miss you most of all because I always wanted to be extra close to you and have the fun that two brothers should have.

Dad, I heard everything you had to say to me even though I already know what's happening. I'll do my best to please you and make you proud of me.

And finally, Mom, I know you'll be praying. Don't stop, because it makes me very proud to know that I still have a mother that cares enough about her son to ask God to help him. Don't worry so much about me; actually I'm not that bad a person. Maybe this time, Mom, I'll make it.

How much I think of you all and love you, you'll never really know. But I do! If you think I'm running away from responsibility, you're wrong. It's taking much more courage to fight this alone than to stay here in this nice set-up and make it with your help. I'll miss you all.

Love,
Ralph

P.S. It's great to have two new sisters to live in my home. It's your job now, Moa and Becky, to take care of Mom and pull her apron strings while I'm gone.

Harold scraped the ice off the windshield while the car reluctantly sputtered to a start. We followed the bend around the lake to Friendly Road. There he was, shoulders hunched in the fleece-lined jacket we had given him for Christmas, and apparently hiking to the airport.

With my flannel nightgown tailing under my coat, I jumped out of the car and ran to him. Frantically holding him,

I pleaded desperately for him to come home. Dan and Harold put their arms around Ralph and quietly persuaded him into the warm car. He was shivering with the cold, and with the uncertainty of his life.

Dan started a fire in the fireplace and I grilled cheese sandwiches and heated cocoa with marshmallows floating on the top. Too spent for words, we sat by the fire. Although our love and concern folded Ralph in a mantle, he remained cold, and I knew that it was only a matter of time before he would leave again.

At last the warmth of the fire and food made us sleepy and I followed the boys upstairs. I sat beside Ralph and stroked his hair, singing childhood lullabies and praying for warm memories to return again. Even in his sleep he rolled and tossed, but I stayed, humming and trying to soothe the restlessness within him. Finally I knelt by his bed and sobbed quietly and prayed. He slept fitfully. Dan was sound asleep in his bed. Harold was torn between hate and love: hate for the destruction he saw and love for his son.

I wrapped a blanket around me and sat by the window, afraid to go to bed for fear he would leave again. Although I knew I couldn't hold him back, I could, perhaps, delay the inevitable. The fire was dying out. The lake below glistened with snow. The house was still, and I sat, numb with fear. The blanket around me couldn't keep out the icy clutches of doubt about the year ahead.

It was January 1, 1970.

7

Unclog the Channel

It was a cold January morning when I walked into the college infirmary to turn on the lights and heat before Lena arrived. From the backroads of my memory came the dean's booming voice, "Well, Florence Nightingale, you must be living right. Meet Lena Rogers." That was two years ago. Little had he realized that from the kitchen classroom Lena would be teaching her own brand of philosophy, in addition to preparing trays and making beds. The students loved her—especially her "Lena tea" and cheese sandwiches. I loved her—Lena—a symphony in black.

While the steam radiators clanged and hissed, I reached for the coffeepot. At 6:30 A.M., the world outside was still wrapped in darkness just like me. Outwardly I was the starched infirmary nurse, but inside I was broken from grief over our youngest son who had chosen the "rebellion of the sixties," instead of an education in a fine Christian college.

I heard Lena coming up the sidewalk, singing into the cold wind—

We walk by faith
And not by sight
We move one step at the time
Thy Word's a lamp
Thy Word's a light
We move one step at the time.

The door banged open with a "Praise the Lord, Sister Jensen, we got us a brand new day. The Lord done give it to us and the devil ain't gonna take it away. Glory!" She stopped with: "Lord have mercy, child, you look like death."

"I might as well be dead! No way I can live with this grief. Janice, Daniel, and Ralph were inseparable as children, and now Ralph is wandering in a wilderness of drugs and protests. I can't live without Ralph in the fold."

Lena reached for the broom and hollered, "Out, Satum— Out! No devil gonna be in my kitchen. You trying to kill my child—and no way you can win! Out! Out! In the name of Jesus!" She swept with a fury through the open door and announced, "Now that we got rid of the devil, we can hear from God."

She gathered me in her arms and I brushed my face against her black cheek and sobbed, "I might as well be dead." With that, Lena straightened her shoulders and looked at me with those black eyes and said words that turned a light on inside me. "If God had wanted you to die for Ralph, He would have asked you! You standing there telling God Almighty He not done enough for your child. That's what the cross am all about. Jesus died for Ralph. He came that you might have life, that your joy might be full. Now I asks you, where is your joy?"

"But Lena, I want my son saved!"

"Your joy got nothin' to do with what you wants. Your joy am Jesus, child! You got Him, you got peace. You got Him, you got it all! Ralph not your business. He is God's business. Now I ask you, did the prodigal son's father call in the FBI or the police? No. He trusted God, and he waited. Now, Sister Jensen, you must *unclog the channel.* You get the long hair, bare feet, drugs, and that mess out that channel so you can see God. God's getting tired of hearing how bad the boy looks. He's lookin' in the heart. Now today we get the joy! First, I takes authority. Lord. we don't want no phone calls, no sick calls in this here infirmary until we gets the joy business settled. Thank You, Jesus. O Lord, this child don't know how to praise. Forgive her, Lord." She rolled her black eyes heavenward and grabbed me under my arm and marched me around the infirmary. "We begins to praise the Lord till the joy comes."

I sobbed as we started singing the "Doxology," and then Lena prodded, "Walk, child, walk! March, keep marching. The devil don't like marching—ever since those Jericho walls came tumbling down. We got some walls to march around. Now sing, 'Power in the Blood,' and pat your hands. Satum hates that clappin'. Keep walking child. Hold your head up. You is a child of the King. Thank God for everything—that your child is in God's hands."

When I sat down to rest, she picked up the worn Bible and read back to me the promises I had marked for her. She pulled up a chair beside me and sang, "Oh, how I love Jesus." We harmonized together as the tears rolled and hearts were raised in worship. We sang softly, "Holy, holy, holy, Lord God Almighty—All Thy works shall praise Thy name."

"Take off your shoes. We are standing on holy ground." Quietly we slipped off our shoes and fell to our knees singing, "His name is Wonderful." "For Thou alone art worthy." We bowed in humble adoration.

"Don't see the problem—just see Jesus," she prodded. "Let the joy of the Lord be your strength. Thank You Jesus for searching for our lamb," she sobbed. "He done lost his way, but You can find him." Then, "Up, up, Sister Jensen. We now offer the sacrifice of praise!"

We had started with a sobbing "Doxology," and two hours later we ended with a victorious, "Praise the Lord." Rejoicing, I wrote in my diary, "I won't be any happier the day Ralph comes home than I am today receiving the answer in my spirit, by my faith."

Lena looked out across the busy campus and stretched her arms to heaven. "Thank You, Jesus. We done birthed a child in the Spirit."

Not until the close of Lena's prayer did the phone ring and the doors bang. The coffeepot stayed warm.

8

His Eye Is on the Sparrow

The cracking of the woodcutter's ax mingled with the wind blowing through the Massachusetts winter forest made Ralph's arms ache endlessly. He was alternating between hot and cold, and he shivered in the wind. He knew he was sick, but he forced his arms and legs to move with the ax.

While his body moved in automatic rhythm, his mind was free to remember. Blurred images from the past floated before his burning eyes. He swung at the logs, for it was forgetting he needed, not remembering. But the memory insisted.

He had convinced his childhood friend, Billy Welker, to join him in Massachusetts. Through the years they had made similar choices. They knew their mothers prayed, and secretly they were thankful. Perhaps, one day, they would come back, but gradually the tide of the times was pulling them out to sea.

Ralph thought ruefully, *Yeah, Billy got to go to East Carolina University, but I had to go to a Christian college. They called me "cornbread and grits" ... well, I showed them, those Yankees, that's not all a southern boy is ... but what I wouldn't give for some country ham and grits right now.*

His stomach was empty. He showed those Yankees—huh—fell right in with all the protests and anti-war sentiment. He sure was glad nothing had happened to his brother Dan in Vietnam. Dan was too good to die. It was different with him, though, he had already died to ambition and self-worth. He was part of that so-called enlightenment his friends talked about. He was "enlightened" all right! His eyes were opened to a world of nightmare and fantasy. The things that were—looked unreal. The unreal became the norm.

He had always wanted a girl like his sister, Jan, warm and fun-loving, and a good Christian. But he'd only found her opposite. How was he to know those limpid eyes and that warm mouth in a hazy dream world would lead to mere sensual warmth?

He thought about the T.V. commercial, "Bet you can't eat just one." That's how it was, one more drink, one high, another hazy dream world of soft nights. He felt as though he had been on skis—faster and faster down the snowy slopes, wild with excitement, biting wind—faster—faster—and then his clenched fist pounded into the tree. In fury he thrust his ax into another log.

He was finished! Expelled from school—and he couldn't go home in defeat. He needed a job—and then what?

Maybe the cook at the college would give him something to eat and maybe he could sneak into the dorm. At least it would be warm. He was so tired, and his throat hurt. *Strep throat, probably.*

He remembered the night after he'd left school, when the gang had talked about home, and someone had asked, "Ralph, why do you stay here?"

"I don't know. That's just it—I don't know where I belong." Then he remembered why he couldn't go home. He had seen those horrible demons coming at him, and the devil laughing at him. "No hope for you—too late—too late. You can never go home again!" Somehow he believed it. There were no more girls like Jan—they were all treacherous, like quicksand. There would be no more picnics or talks around the table. He didn't know what he wanted to do—maybe wander around the world and take his happiness where he found it.

Wish Mom were here to do something for this throat—a bowl of chicken noodle soup, cocoa with marshmallows—sure do miss Jo Jo, the beagle—but they'll get used to being without me.

How he detested those long letters from Mom—endless sermons on challenges, potential, and wasting one's life. She should know—but, then again, he did hate to hurt her. Dad was never there when he needed him—always on the road. Besides he bragged about Jan and Dan, and had everyone "pray for Ralph."

He was remembering the time Billy Welker and he got picked up in Greensboro and the policeman gave a warning, "If I were you, I wouldn't hurt your father, Ralph; he does so much good." *How come he didn't have time for me?* he wondered, but then again he remembered how Dad prayed for him at college and was so proud of him. "We'll make up for lost time, Son, and have some great times together."

Jan, married to a good, all-right guy—one terrific sister, that gal. Then Dan—always doing the right thing, yet, he made me feel like a dumb kid. And Mom, good grief, she idolized Dan—and only prayed for me. Heck, who wants to be prayed for? I'd rather be loved. I really didn't want to hurt anyone, but it's too late now. They all will have the farm and all their dreams. Who wants me?

That darn throat! I'm so cold and hungry. Why do I always think of Mom when I'm cold and hungry? Why does she write such long letters? Oh, well—I told her to send the weather report.

*I wonder what Dad would say if he knew how Billy and I used
to play poker in the balcony during church services?*

He chuckled to himself—but then darkness engulfed
him; the misty panorama of the past swam into focus and his
two years of college played before him like a horror movie.

Deep insecurity and low self-esteem had smouldered
into defiance at being pressured into attending a Christian
school. The only southern boy in the northern school, along
with being labeled "grits and cornbread," he also was called
a "barefooted moonshiner."

So he determined to play out the whole southern-boy
role. Turning on the charm, he sought out and influenced
other rebellious students, and they formed the YAC Club—
Young Americans for the Confederacy. Eventually these New
England "rebels" joined the rebel yell of the Confederates.

There was that day at Gordon, when they tore down the
American flag and raised the flag of the Confederacy. Another
day, Ralph found himself among hundreds of protestors at
the Boston Commons, waiting to hear the liberal political
platforms of the Boston Moratorium speakers. But disillusion-
ment reigned. Even the rebellious hippies, resenting the at-
tacks against their homeland, booed the speakers. In those
days the United States was experiencing a lot of conflict and
confusion—both internally and externally.

Ralph was confused too. He felt rage against deserters
fleeing to Canada and Sweden, but at the same time, he resented the war. Groping for reasons for his anger, he experi-
enced the lingering pain of injustices—the Greensboro sit-in,
the Kent State tragedy, and the anti-war hysteria.

From the midst of this confusion the drug culture emerged,
promising a temporary escape from life's harsh realities. Ex-
perimenting with drugs dulled the pain.

Branded a racist and a rebel, Ralph justified his actions
by judging certain things. He saw cruelty being expressed by

some of the black students—through a deliberate blow to the eye of a football player or an unnecessarily cracked skull.

One night, he was walking with a girl on the edge of the campus, and they were approached by a group of blacks. One of the blacks made an obscene remark to the girl. She was horrified, and in a burst of fury, Ralph clenched his fists and attacked the leader. Fortunately, the others pulled them apart.

Later, when a black girl angrily railed at the black male students for making advances toward the white girls and passing by their own kind, Ralph loudly applauded on the sidelines.

During this time, concerned school officials were seriously attempting to establish campus unity, and several black students from foreign countries had blended into college life. These students demonstrated a deep dedication to the Lord and a significant purpose for living. Their mutual acceptance was evident.

But when Gordon College opened its doors to inner city Spanish and black students, the YAC Club continually tried to disrupt peaceful relationships. Harassment and intimidation became popular weapons.

Ralph had started out by playing a part, but soon his deep, genuine resentment surfaced. On one particular Homecoming Day, one of the parade floats portrayed a huge black hand clasped with a white hand. The theme was "Unity." The explosive rebellion deep within Ralph screamed, "Never!" And in his rage, he set fire to the float. His action incited other rebels; a riot began and a number of the other floats also were set afire.

The floats were artificial, made of paper—but the anger was alarmingly real. Tensions began mounting over other issues, and it was inevitable that Ralph would be expelled.

Chuckling to himself again, he relived one winter night when the brazen rebels defied even the weather. Dressed only in combat boots and underwear shorts, they marched around the campus, and, encouraged by the cheers from the girls' dormitory, they dove into three feet of snow.

Ironically, by the time he reached his last semester, he had a thirst for knowledge, and a longing to return to serious study—but it was too late. He had exceeded the school's grace and mercy. Payday had arrived.

Some of the inner-city students who were on cocaine also were expelled from school. (Rebellion knows no color. The heart of every man is deceitful.)

Nothing seemed to erase Ralph's deep loneliness, nor the haunting memories, which kept coming, like recurring nightmares. *Maybe it was all wrong,* he thought now, *but everyone told me, "Do your own thing—be free."*

The past continued to parade by him with its aura of bitterness and anger. He felt that every segment of society was to blame—home, church, and school.

But now, he had broken away from society's restraints of discipline. Now, he was finally free to sail his own ship. Yes, he was the captain of his own fate.

Nuts. It's getting dark and I can't chop any more wood, and, gosh, I hurt all over. What a rotten world! It's suppertime at home, and I'll bet Mom has meatballs and mashed potatoes and maybe my favorite cherry pie. Oh, well, they probably don't think about me, except that stupid prayer meeting at the Masons. I can hear Dorothy now, "We must all remember to pray for Ralph." Well—let them pray! It won't do any good, but I sure am hungry—and it's so cold.

The woods seemed dark and lonely as Ralph picked up the ax for the final blow. Suddenly across the trees the wind brought a song. He could hear Ethel Waters singing—"His eye is on the sparrow and I know He watches me." He couldn't remember the whole verse.

That's the record Mom played over and over at home! For a moment he was afraid—the wind, the evening darkness, the cold and hot flashes, and that insistent aching.

He stood still in the shadows and the wind carried the song again:

> His eye is on the sparrow
> And I know He watches me.

"O.K., O.K.," he screamed into the wind, "God, if you really watch over me, then give me a ride to Gordon College—and a job!"

In desperation he picked up his ax and went out to the road to thumb a ride to Wenham.

Half mocking, half afraid, he waited.

A black Cadillac pulled up and a woman's voice called out, "Need a ride, young man? I'm going to Wenham." In a daze, Ralph got into the car with a "Thank you, Ma'am." (They always laughed at his southern Sir and Ma'am.) Well, let them laugh—he *was* a southerner.

They rode in silence until the driver said, "Young man, I'm in need of a man to work on my estate. Are you interested in a job? I'll have a big breakfast waiting for you. Agreed? 8 A.M. it will be!"

Late that night the phone rang in Greensboro. "Hello, Mom, it's Ralph. I have a job tomorrow, but I have a bad sore throat. Would you—?" After a pause, I answered, "Of course, Ralph, I'll pray for you."

Unknown to Ralph, miles away, two hands were clasped in prayer—one was white, the other was black.

9

A Waiting Time

The Greensboro College infirmary door opened with a familiar voice calling out, "Where's Lena?"

"Dan boy, Lena right here in the kitchen. Where else?" she laughed. "I saw you coming up the drive and I said, 'There comes our Vietnam boy—home safe and sound. Thank You, Jesus.' Go tell your mama to stop for a cup of tea."

With a bear hug for Lena and me, Dan joined us for a cup of tea and oven toast.

"Seems like I feels a restless spirit, so you better tell Lena what be troubling your soul."

"I just don't know what to do." Dan stretched his long legs and threw up his hands. "I had an offer to teach in the mountains because the present teacher is moving to another state—right in the middle of a school year. I have to give an answer today. Then there is a possibility of a better financial offer with a pharmaceutical company, but I won't be sure about that job for another week. The salesman job sounds better, but the teaching job is sure. Then again, Lena, I've been thinking so much about the dream I had in Vietnam about buying land. I sensed such a need to have land and build homes for all the family, to be independent, you know—water supply, gardens, animals, and even a windmill. It seems so important to be self-sufficient. We shouldn't be so dependent upon foreign oil, and we need to take care of each other. O.K., Lena. That means you come with us. I have so much on my mind and so many decisions to make."

"Now Dan, this Lena learn a long time ago we do one thing at a time. Dreams and visions be good. God tells folks in dreams and visions, but folks got to learn to wait on the Lord for the right time. Sometimes we tells secrets when God says to ponder in the heart. Now, you have no money, so how you buy land? First thing, you get a job. Now what you got in your hand?"

"The teaching job, Lena."

"My spirit says what you find in your hand—do it. You best get on that telephone and you tell that bossman you start teaching Monday. That be in your hand."

Within moments the restlessness was gone, and a peace filled the room. Dan picked up the phone, "Yes sir, I'll be there Monday morning."

"Now that we got that out of the hand, so we puts the next thing in the hand, and that be the land. You get ready for your new job and I'll be stretching out before the Lord about the land. Some things takes a knowing, and some things takes a stretching. This land be a stretching out kind, and that takes time. 'They wait upon the Lord shall run.' Most folks run before the waiting. I learn to wait before running. The Word say, 'Stand still and see.'[1] Now I asks you how much you see, running? You sees best when standing. Now where you stand? I stands on the Word, the promises of God—then I see."

With a chuckle Lena added, "I has to watch for your mama. She likes running better than standing. When Friday comes I tell her, 'Now stop organizing the weekend and trust God to work all things for good.' "

It was good to have Dan home. Harold was on the road most of the time. Ralph had returned to his friends in Massachusetts. Janice was busy with her new baby in Michigan. There was an emptiness in the house. Now Dan was home and we took long walks by the lake and Dan shared the dream about the farm. Sometimes he had me doubled up laughing while he told stories from his classroom in the mountains. We read the Bible and prayed together, and asked God's guidance about the farm, a place of refuge for the family and God's people.

Late into the night I relived the dream I had written down on my fortieth birthday. That dream was for a farm for the children and grandchildren. "There would always be a place to come home to," identified the desire of my heart.

Perhaps the dream originated in Canada when I was a child. My love for the open prairie and the waving wheat fields stayed with me through the years of Chicago with its clamor and skyscrapers.

I was reliving my childhood and the wind on the Canadian prairie. I could feel Dolly's silver mane against my face as we galloped the country road, and heard again my own words, "Dolly, I love you, and I'll remember this moment forever." I did!

Into my memory came the discordant sound of elevated trains near a second-floor flat in Chicago. My escape was a return to the backroads of my mind where the dream lingered—of land, woods, valleys, streams, gardens, and the wind in the valley.

In the meantime, my sister Doris Hammer from Winston-Salem had been praying about the same dream—an all-encompassing dream that included the extended family. To some of the family, New Yorkers, it seemed more like a nightmare than a dream.

"Child, don't you never learn that the secrets of the Lord are secrets, and not to be talked about before time?"

Lena's admonition came often, because we forgot, in our enthusiasm, to "wait, sit, and stand still." "Waiting come before running and standing before seeing. Now is the waiting time."

Dan, Doris, and I placed a map before us, and prayed for guidance.

Lena stretched out before the Lord—and waited.

10

The Sound of Music

"Be anxious for nothing, Sister Jensen, and don't be fretting about the day God answers. He done answered, but it take time to get the answer through. We best keep praying with thanksgiving and believing. The begging and the pleading be done in heaven. God get so tired of all that begging when He tells us over and over, 'It is finished!' Why we beg more than we believe?

"When folks come up to you and say, so sad like, 'How is Ralph?' now just smile and say, 'My Ralph, he be fine.' When folks say, 'Where is he?' you say, 'I don't know, but I know he is fine because we put him in God's hands. He is fine!

"When you go to that Mason prayer meeting, you just stop begging everyone to pray for Ralph. You tell folks to join you to praise God for he is fine. Those coonching spirits of doubt and unbelief stop more prayers than we know! I hates those coonching spirits! Now we wait for God and not be running so much. We ask the spirit of joy, peace, love, and thanksgiving to fill our hearts and this infirmary.

"O Glory—thank You, Jesus, our child be coming home.

We leave the day to You, Lord Jesus, but we wait with believing.

"I best go with you to the prayer meeting. No more crying and begging for Ralph. Prayers get answered with praising. You told me yourself how that king got the folks together and put the choir up front to march to the enemy line. How come you forget so soon?"

I reached for my Bible—2 Chronicles 20: "'Jehoshaphat feared, and set himself to seek the Lord, and proclaimed a fast—neither know we what to do, but our eyes are upon Thee—then the spirit of the Lord came upon Jahaziel—Thus saith the Lord unto you, Be not afraid nor dismayed at this great multitude; for the battle is not yours but God's. Stand still, and see the salvation of the Lord.' "[1]

"Hallelujah," shouted Lena, "What I be telling you—stand still and see! Now I know the rest: that king got to believing that prophet and he said, 'Get that choir together—never mind practicing—you just march down that valley. You be singing, "Power in the Blood" and "Victory in Jesus," and pat your hands and stomp them coonching spirits of unbelief and doubt. You sing with all your heart, and you sing, "In the name of Jesus we have the victory." ' I know what happened. That enemy heard all that shouting and praising and it sounded like ten armies coming after them. They got so full of fear and the Lord put His army of ministering spirits behind the bushes and the enemy got so mixed up they killed each other. I figure that is why the choir sings before the preacher preaches. The choir starts praising God and the spirits of unbelief and doubt gets mixed up and leaves so folks can hear the preaching. Tonight I get Lucille to come with me and we go to the prayer meeting to sing praises, and stand still and see. Now we best get our work done."

When the day came to a close I pulled into the driveway with a new expectancy in my heart.

The house was quiet as Harold was out of town, and I finished the household duties quickly. Before I realized it, I was dressed, and on my way to the home of Mr. and Mrs. Mason, and their daughter, Dorothy Weymann, and a granddaughter, Margaret Weymann.

The Tuesday night prayer meeting had begun twenty-five years ago as a family night, then others joined to pray for their families. The Masons' prayer meeting included a time of special prayer for their older daughter, Miriam Talley, who, with her husband Joe and their two children, traveled around the world preaching the gospel and giving sacred concerts.

Each week organ, piano, violin, or accordion music played by Dorothy Weymann poured forth across the affluent suburban area of Greensboro.

It was not the music alone that drew the people, but the man, Mr. Mason.

This godly, white-haired man reached out his hand, from a heart of compassion, and lifted the people to God.

No problem was too big or too small for his listening heart. His prayers touched the heart of God and reached into the hidden corners of each life.

During the night hours he communed with God. He was no mystical spiritist, but a loving, humorous, brilliant man who bent his intellect and ability toward the wisdom of God.

The sick, the fearful, the lonely and the sinful came to his door, all assured of love without condemnation. The rebellious young came on bare feet, holding in their hands the mess of pottage for which they had sold their birthright.

They left with their feet shod with the gospel of peace and clothed in the righteousness of God.

The broken hearts came, too wounded to weep, so Mr. Mason wept for them until the healing came. The defeated came too beaten to stand, so he sat with them until together they stood.

Then I came, and Mr. Mason waited with me until the answer came.

Cars were parked down the street when I arrived, but I walked with the others to the sound of the music wafting into the night. My sister, Doris, from Winston-Salem often joined me, and tonight Lena and Lucille would come.

We never knew who the visiting guests might be. Missionaries and ministers from around the world visited the prayer meeting at the Masons' home. My dear friend from High Point, North Carolina, Frances Dalton, seldom missed, and she often brought missionaries and musicians, some from England or the Philippines, to share their music and experiences. Each night was a special event.

No one wanted to go home. Testimonies spontaneously sprouted and prayer and praise ascended to the throne.

"Never thought I'd see white folks praising God like black folks," said Lena. "God got so tired of all them fences folks put up so He just let His spirit jump over the fences and then His people pulled down the gates that shut them in and all got together at this prayer meeting. Glory to Jesus!"

Mr. Mason opened our eyes to the Word: "Keep yourselves little children. Look to Jesus, the author and finisher of your faith. Hold fast to that which is good. Don't be led away by strange devices.[2]

"This is a filling station—a place to receive go-power, strength and joy. A place to pray together—to believe together. Little children," he urged, "be faithful where God has put you—in your church, in your home, at work. Be salt. Be a light. Meditate on the Word of God. Seek the Giver, Jesus—not gifts, but Him. He will freely give you all things. Love one another—don't condemn. Jesus loves you."

The words lingered long in the hearts of the people, especially in the hearts of the young. They may have rejected tradition, but no one rejected the love of this godly man. To me he was the gentle father I had never known. I loved this man of God.

The meeting was over. We stood to sing. All around the living room, kitchen, hall, and stairway the young and old joined hands and sang—

> Only believe,
> Only believe...

Mr. Mason's benediction ended with the song—

> O how I love Jesus
> Because He first loved me.

I said goodnight to Lena and we went to our separate homes, but we both carried in our hearts the sound of music.

11

Shalom Valley

I heard her singing across the campus before she opened the door to the infirmary.

"Sister Jensen, the Lord done give us a new day and no debbil can take it away. We not be keeping no coonching spirits around this infirmary. I just tell all doubts to leave right now in the name of Jesus. We unclogged the channel and God gave us a knowing and we birthed that child in the Spirit. Nothing make me and you doubt!"

"Oh, Lena, sometimes I feel the waves of despair rolling over me and I almost sink, but I put my hand on the Bible every night and tell the whole world, 'This is where I stand—on the Word of God.' I read my verse out loud—Isaiah 49:25: '...I will save thy children,' and I just shout it out that I am a believer, not a doubter."

"Ha—you learning, child. Nothing wrong with the waves of despair rolling over you. A big ship on the ocean pays no never mind to the waves beating against the ship. But just let one little wave get inside and watch those sailor-boys get to work.

"We has to do the same—keeps the waves outside, Sister

Jensen. But if one little coonching spirit of doubt sneak in, you better get those praising spirits busy to get that doubt.

"When you births a baby, it takes nine months to birth him for folks to see, but that baby be birthed inside and growing where God can see. How you know that birthing is done on the inside? When the time comes we see that boy come into the world, naked, yelling, and hungry. I tell you, Sister Jensen, our boy will come birthed again—hollering, naked, and hungry. We be there to feed him and clothe him and we'll all cry out to God together. That day coming. Now is the waiting time. Now be the time to wait on the Lord and rest in the Lord and He already done promised to bring it to pass. Know why we be so sure? My Jesus not willing for no one to perish, and, when we pray in His will, He hears and answers. This is His will and He gives us a knowing. God not in a hurry. He knows what He is doing.

"God rested on the seventh day. He just finished creating everything and if that had been me and you, most likely we would have organized all we did those six days. Sometimes God says, 'Sit down child. Take the weight off your feet and start believing in your heart.'

"Remember the day in January when we got the joy of the Lord and unclogged the channel? Remember how I used to get the newspaper every morning, but that morning, when we got the glory in this infirmary, the Lord talk to me on the way to work. He said, 'Lena, you won't have time to read the paper today. From now on you study My Word and I will open your eyes.'

"I had my piece of money in my hand, but I put it away and came to work without the paper. That day God gave us His word, and a knowing.

"Now this morning when I came to work, the Lord said, 'Lena, buy a paper today. I have something to show you.' So here is the paper and I'll ask the Lord to show me what He wants me to see. But first we have coffee and a piece of toast."

I returned to my office and forgot the newspaper. The day demanded my full attention, until later in the afternoon.

The newspaper was open to the "Land For Sale" section, and Lena had circled: 66 ACRES FOR SALE, Stoneville, North Carolina.

"This is what the Lord showed me," added Lena, "and we best tell Dan boy."

I opened my Bible and read: "With arrows and with bows shall men come thither; because all the land shall become briers and thorns" (Isaiah 7:24).

We went to see the property.

"Appears to me the land is scrub pine and good for hunting," I commented.

Briers, thorns, and thistles made hiking an adventure in endurance. Dan used a machete to cut a path to the spring where clear mountain water ran freely. The old cabin built some 200-years ago out of hand-hewn logs was filled with old debris. The wind sighed through the pines and the whippoorwills called out a welcome. Evening was settling over the valley.

In my journal I wrote: "The solid fabric of the universe hangs on His eternal arm.

"Traverse the lonely valley where rocks enclose you on either side, rising like battlements to heaven. You might be the only traveler in the lonely glen, where a bird darts up afraid, or the moss trembles under foot. But God is there, revealing His wonders in a thousand ways:

> filling the tiny buttercup with the fragrance of
>   His perfume;
> upholding the rocky barriers with His mighty
>   arm;
> refreshing the lonely pine with the breath of His
>   mouth.

"Descend with me to the ocean depths, where undisturbed the waters sleep, the very sand motionless in unbroken quiet. God is there—revealing His existence in the silent palace of the sea."[1]

Could it be that God was in my silent palace of seemingly unanswered prayer?

12

What for Your Mama Pay Tuition?

This was the day for the athletes' routine physicals. The doctor would be here any moment and I hurriedly had the history sheets ready, with height, weight and blood pressure recorded. Everyone was in a jovial mood and kept urging Lena to sing. Lena, always a ham at heart, put on a good show to the delight of the waiting students.

She turned to the other students, waiting for medicine or excuse slips, and asked one of the girls, "What for your mama pay tuition?"

"Oh, I'm a music major."

"You hear that children? Her mama pay tuition for her to study music. Now sing Lena a song."

"I can't sing, Lena, I just study music so I can teach, or direct, and perhaps compose."

Lena sat quietly. "You can't sing? Surely child, you got a song in the heart. No tuition pay for that. I got a song in my heart that be a gift—no tuition. I got to sing the song in my heart or it be gone."

A chorus went up, "Come on Lena, another song."

She closed her eyes and sang: "Without Him I would be nothing..."

It was quiet and then Lena turned to a tall boy, "What for your mama pay tuition?"

"I'm majoring in economics."

"Oh, so that be like add and take away, like gain and loss."

"Well, yes, in a way, Lena. Economics is the study of laws affecting production, distribution, and consumption of wealth."

"That be like that man in the Bible. He produced so much grain he told his servants to help him build bigger barns. Only thing, the Lord had different kind of economics. The Lord be studying how to build a bigger man. 'For what shall it profit a man, if he gain the whole world, and lose his own soul?'[1]

"God wants a bigger man to put His Son inside, because with Him you can do anything. Without Him, boy, you got big barns, but a mighty small man. Do your teacher tell you about that kind of gain and loss?

"Oh, oh, here comes that doctor. I best be getting him a cup of tea.

"He look plumb wore out. When I go home tonight I'll cook him a pound cake and bring it to his office. You young'uns best be proud to have a good doctor. He take good care of you."

With a knowing look of warning to be good, Lena retreated to the kitchen and closed the door.

Tony was sitting at the table with his curly black-haired head down on his arms—a picture of utter despair.

"Lena, I'm in trouble!"

"That not be new around here, boy. You been asking for trouble, so why you not happy to get it?"

"Oh, Lena, don't be mad. I know I goofed, but now my uncles from New York are coming and I'll be taken out of school."

"You best go to that dean man and tell him you be mighty sorry and promise to study hard. Before you go, you get that silly hair off your neck and take a good shower. Then don't go in no bare feet—and get some nice clothes on you and get that foolish mustache off that hangs down your chin. You got a smart head, but your brains run ahead of good sense. You nothing but a baby, trying to act so big. You be about the youngest one in school, too smart for your own good . . . and your uncles from New York so proud of you. They pay tuition so you can make your papa and mama proud. They come from the old country and work in the mill. Your papa got so many babies, and you be the first to go to college. You going to let those big playboys in the dormitory tell you how to live your life? You let those smart girls, who sneak in the boys' rooms, pay your tuition? You not been out of diapers too long and not too long ago you nothing but a little fat baby drinking milk from your mama.

"Who worked at the mill to buy that spaghetti to feed ten young'uns? Who be so proud because you be so smart you can skip grades and come to college so young? Your brains done skipped grades, but your common sense still be in kindergarten.

"You grew up with brothers and sisters and you all got dumped in the tub together, and you know what girls look like. They change a little and get more like your mama, and boys just get more like the papa. So what need to study so much about girls?

"God makes girls every day and God makes boys every day. The pattern don't change. You boys slipping around like you don't know what girls are made of. You all know what girls look like. Looking at all those picture books you hide under the bed, you find something new? Ha!

"You best go now and come by here to show how you be dressed. The dean is a big man and you show respect—hear?"

Lena watched Tony amble across campus, shoulders drooping with despair. "O Lord, I be calling out his name again, Tony be so young. He always had his mama and papa and all those young'uns at home. Now he feels ashamed. Help him do right. He used to go to a priest, but I comes to You, Jesus. You be my priest and plead my case and all these young'uns You gave me. They needs to know You so they be doing their own praying, but I'll keep calling out their name so they can know You like I do. Help all those smart teachers who know so many books, but don't know Your Book, Lord. O my Jesus, if they just know You, the Holy Spirit will lead them into all truth. I don't know what be in that big library, but I asks You to help me know Your Book. Everything I need to know be right here in Your Word. I thank You, Jesus, I can read, and what I don't understand Your Spirit can teach me. Thank You, Jesus!"

"Hey, Lena!"

The kitchen door banged open and a gangling youth grabbed Lena around the waist. "I just changed my major. I'm going into social science."

Lena, laughing, poured a cup of tea and asked, "And what be that, child?"

"Well, it is the science or the art of dealing with human society—family, state, race. I believe we can make changes in our society—to reduce poverty, eliminate crime, and end discrimination. Lena, I want to be a part of that change. We are organizing a march."

"Well, praise the Lord, child! The march I knows the most about was the march around Jericho. Those walls come plumb down. Glory to Jesus!

"I marches most every day! Early in the morning I takes my Bible and I marches around this infirmary and stomp down them walls of sin and pride and hate. I marches around the walls of rebellion against God's way. I cry out to Jesus to get love and obedience in the hearts. I sing, 'Power in the Blood' and pat my hands and get a beat in my feet. That Satum hate that marching.

"We marched around our church too. Our preacher told the young'uns, 'Any marching to do, you all march right to this here altar and gets your heart right before you getting other folks right.' "

"Oh, come on Lena, that's not the kind of marching I mean. I'm talking about a march for justice and equality—for people's rights."

"Now you talking, boy, we be talking about the same thing—people's rights.

" 'There be a way that seems right to a man, but the end is death,'[2] Jesus said. 'I am the way, the truth, and the life: no man cometh unto the Father, but by Me.'[3] Now God gave man the right to choose. He can choose God's way or man's way. I get so mad at that Satum, I just stomp him under my feet. That devil gets folks doing everything else except choosing the right way. He gets folks stirred up about the blacks and the white folks. There be more hate now than before. God says, 'Love one another,' and that means black, red, yellow, and white. Now, I ask you, what you see in this infirmary? Who passed laws that make Lena love Nurse Jensen, and who told Nurse Jensen she has to love me? That comes when we choose to love God first and then obey, 'Love one another.' "[4]

"But Lena, what about poverty?"

"God says, 'Give and it shall be given.'[5] Now I'll tell you one thing, I've never seen the righteous forsaken, or His seed begging bread. God will supply our need. We needs a thankful heart—not begging for T-bone steaks when God supplies the turnip salad and cornbread. Ever hear how Nurse Jensen grew up in Canada when her papa was a missionary to the folks coming over to this country? Nurse Jensen had oatmeal three times a day and thought she was rich. She be rich in thanksgiving—that's what be rich.

"Folks want everything the rich folks have, without working for it. What the rich folks don't know is they be poor in spirit, poor in joy and thanks, poor in love, and mighty poor in peace. They frets more over that money. Then again the people working for the rich folks have to stomp on them coonching spirits of envy and covetousness and be thankful for work and be praising God for their salvation. They be the rich ones. God help us all to know what we got and not be marching for something we already have.

"What country in the world give us such freedom?

"Do you see folks going in boats and ships and planes to get into Russia? Now I asks you—How come folks risking their lives to come to America if it be so bad? Why aren't they begging to get into Russia or Cuba? What they eat over there, T-bone steaks? All these smart lawyers, taking prayer out of school! Huh—Why they not go to live in Russia if they don't want prayer? Then ask the folks in Russia how they like to have a Bible and a songbook. They be mighty proud to carry a Bible and a songbook.

"People be mean to people since they be born. Cain killed his own brother Abel. Took some time for God to straighten out Joseph and his brothers. It's not black folk and white folk, child, it just be folk. 'All have sinned and come short of the glory of God.' That's the Bible, child—and don't you start telling me you don't believe the Bible. Now I don't know nothing about building bridges or any other kind of building, but I smart enough to know there be twelve inches in a foot. When I measures my window for cloth to make my kitchen curtains, I use the same ruler that those big builders use. We got to start with something. To measure, you starts with a ruler. To live, you starts with life—that be God who give life. To learn God's ways, you start with His Book. That's the ruler, boy.

"Look how man be changing rules. God's rules never been changed. Mighty old rules since Moses be getting those ten commandments.

"Here come all those good-looking boys that be needing a glass of tea. They looks like they could win any kind of a game. They be out there running around the campus to get good strong legs."

"Hey, Lena, Doc says we're very sick and need a glass of Lena's medicine—a sure cure for anything!"

"That's a smart doctor. I even get some cookies to go with it. I watch you running in the morning and I'm mighty proud of the team. I keep calling out your name so you do your life's running with your eyes on Jesus. You can't look back, and you can't watch people, just go by the Book and keeps your eyes on Jesus."

After the last student left, the kitchen was quiet. We sat down for a cup of tea.

"You be mighty troubled, Nurse Jensen."

"I am, Lena, the doctor had to send a girl home. She was six months pregnant and the boyfriend was a drummer in a rock band. When she called him to tell him about the baby, he said, 'Tough. That's your problem. Get an abortion.' The doctor was furious and told the young man, 'This is America—not Russia. We are talking about your child.' Her father called and sent plane fare for the girl and the drummer to come home. She looked so sad.

"Remember that quiet girl, Lena, the one who worked so hard and now is student teaching and ready to graduate? Well, she decided to have a fling and went to a rock concert—one big blast before graduation. Our doctor sent her to a specialist and she is upstairs with the worst infection he has seen in twenty-five years as a gynecologist. She might not graduate this year. She can't remember what happened—so doped up—but she apparently slept with one boy after another. Her parents are poor and so proud of her. They don't know.

"When I was a student nurse in Cook County Hospital in Chicago, I saw hundreds of babies with venereal disease and infected eyes. I never dreamed I would see anything like this girl in a private church college.

"She's not a bad girl, just thought she was missing some part of life."

"That Satum be so mean. I hates him the way he fool people to make sin so tempting. We have to pray for this girl so she asks God to forgive her for going against His laws and doing her way. That way of man be death. God's way is life."

"Oh, Lena, I don't want Ralph to choose the way of death. Parents work so hard to pay tuition and then we watch young people throw away the very opportunity we would be so thankful to have. May God have mercy on us all, Lena, and grant wisdom to make right decisions."

"Jesus paid big tuition for us to get eternal life. God be watching to see what we do. We best study how we live and trust the rest of the folks to God Almighty."

Lena sang softly:

Jesus paid it all,
All to Him I owe.

Another day had come to a close at Greensboro College infirmary.

13

A Time for Choosing

My dear Ralph,

Praise the Lord! Praise the Lord! We got the property—66 acres for $2,000 down and the rest paid in ten years at 8 percent interest. We all claimed Philippians 4:19, "My God shall supply all your need," and 2 Chronicles 20:20, "Believe in the Lord your God, so shall ye be established." Every step we took has been by the Word of God—even the description of the land.

God will do the same for you, Ralph. He will instruct and teach you. You can get land. All you have to do is trust Him and obey Him.

Read Isaiah 43:25,26. "I, even I, am he that blotteth out thy transgressions for mine own sake, and will not remember thy sins. Put me in remembrance: let us plead together: declare thou, that thou mayest be justified."

Jan sent Dan a book, *Farming in the Bible*. Evelio Perez, our dear friend from Mexico, says the Bible contains wisdom and knowledge for every vocation. All through the Old Testament, God told them and taught them. God taught Noah how to build the ark, and made Abraham the greatest farmer and cattleman. He made Solomon the wisest king, Joshua the greatest soldier, Moses the greatest judge, and on and on!

So, we have made a covenant with God to follow His way and go by His Word, and have dedicated that 66 acres to God and His purpose.

There is one thing I'd like to share with you, and I have told no one else—just you.

All Dad's life he has longed for a little farm, dreamed about it, and talked about it. He finally got enough for a down payment. Like a dream come true. Well, we have been reading the Bible more and listening to tapes.

God starts with the impossible—not the possible. He starts with zero—and makes something. God also has us do something. Remember when Jesus asked the fishermen to "lend Me your boat"? Well, God always asks us to do something—like chess. God moves, we move—step-by-step. So the disciples gave the boat to Jesus—all they possessed.

Remember when Jesus said, "Launch out into the deep," and the disciples filled two boats? You can't out-give God.

Well, back to daddy. His biggest dream was a farm. So now he had $2,000. (I had put $100 down to hold the land.) He gave it all to Jesus—*all he had*—and said, "This is a down payment for the farm and it shall be called Shalom Valley Farm (means Valley of Peace). The title shall be in Dan's and our name as a family farm enterprise."

I am going to work double-duty to buy a truck. That's my boat for Jesus' glory.

Now, Ralph, you have a choice to make, a move in

this game of chess. Move to obey, and give God your will.

We are going to Wild Life (game preserve) tonight for a picnic to celebrate—and then to the farm to start a garden. We're looking for a tractor.

Uncle Gordon called from Brooklyn, New York, and was thrilled about the farm. He's coming to North Carolina. I'm going shopping with Aunt Do.

Believe and you shall receive!

Love,
Mother

Ralph threw the letter in the air with a whoop, and hollered for Rob, Kevin, and Billy to get a load of this news—and the weather report: High, 70 degrees; low, 60 degrees. "That's North Carolina for you," he added gleefully.

"Man, oh, man—a farm! They got the farm! When I was a little kid in kindergarten I drew pictures of horses and farms all the time. I always wanted land—wow! Sixty-six acres! Wow, you guys, there's room for all of us! This I gotta see! Hey, Billy, why don't we hitch a ride to North Carolina?"

The pull from another direction was too great, though, and the question hung in the air like a cloud. Ralph, Rob, Kevin, and Billy were linked together as a family—all out of school.

At times they got together and discussed theology and mockingly reminded each other how they had Sunday school pins for perfect attendance, and Bibles as prizes for memorizing Scripture.

"Maybe we ought to be preachers. We know more about sin and the devil than most preachers." Then a deep depression engulfed them and the mocking laughter died. For a moment they seemed to grasp a light—the farm; then the demonic world of drugs told them they could never go home again. From the cliffs of hope to the valley of despair, their tortured minds wandered in a dry place.

It was cold and rainy the day another letter came from home.

> Dear Ralph,
>
> > High today, 80° and a low of 60°
> >
> > > Love,
> > > Mother

The mocking demons laughed, "Even your mother will forget you. You're all alone, so why don't you marry that little Russian girl? At least you'll belong to someone."

Late one night, Ralph confided to Billy, "Well, somebody ought to help Lee. Her family is all split up and her brother is a communist. She doesn't even believe in God. I bet I could help her. My mom would take her in. The guys treat her like dirt, but Mom would help her."

"What makes you think she wants to change? We aren't changing, are we?"

The darkness came over him again. He had to be alone.

The Atlantic washed up with a constant roar over the rocks off Magnolia's shoreline. Ralph climbed from rock to rock, watching the water splash. Boats and fishermen were out to sea. There was always the pull of the ocean, the dreams that went beyond the horizon. Then memories came with marching feet, hammering blows on his head—never-ending memories, sometimes a blur, sometimes so real that the present was lost and the past regained. Screaming into the wind, he cried to forget, and then he was afraid he would forget.

From his back pocket, Ralph drew out another letter, one he particularly had tried to forget.

My dear Ralph,

Rise up and walk—back to your father's house. Everything you ever longed for is back where you left it. Your work—God's plan for your life—a girl like your sister. Janice.

(O, Lord, how he longed for a girl like Jan—but where were they?)

Even a son—the one you always longed for—a son with your name.
Come back to the road where you made the detour. Come home to your father's house and begin again.
Ralph, in the name of Jesus, rise up and walk—back to your father's house.[1]

We love you,

Mother

The haunting began again—*home? Begin again? Work? What can I do?* One of the verses he had memorized came again, "I will instruct thee and teach thee in the way which thou shalt go. I will guide thee with Mine eye."
Yeah, but I want to do it my way. But where am I going?
A girl like Jan? He sat down and buried his head in his hands while the spray washed over the rocks. The ocean rolled on and on. Such beautiful girls who gave so freely what his sister and others like her guarded jealously for the one man they married. How could he ever deserve a girl like Jan? Besides, he had never met one like her. Jan and Jud were happy and secure. *That's it! That's what I want in a girl, that feeling of a secure love, one to trust and respect. If I could just know she would love me.... Wow! I've sure been looking in the wrong places, yet*

some of these girls come from strict Christian homes. Something's wrong someplace!

Memories washed over his weary mind with haunting scenes of home.

He could see the scrub pine and the trail that he and Dan had cleared at Easter. They hadn't even owned the land, but Lena had said, "Go out there and claim it, in Jesus' name." They did!

Everyone was there—even Jan and baby Heather. Dan cleared a path with the machete and yelled, "Go out there Moses and lead the children across the Red Sea." Ralph remembered the big stick he found, and how, with baby Heather pulling his beard, he led the way down the path. Mom and Doris and the rest followed singing Lena's song:

> Go out there Dan
> Possess the land
> You move one step at the time
> We walk by faith
> And not by sight
> We move one step at the time.

Lena called the trail "the Glory Road" and Highway 220, "the Hallelujah Boulevard." It was April and Easter and he felt like he belonged—and then he decided to go back to Massachusetts to tell his friends. The dream soon became hazy and he was drifting again with his friends in a never-never land.

Then May had come and he decided to hitch a ride to North Carolina to surprise Mom on Mother's Day. He did! He could see them all around the table—Aunt Doris, Uncle Dave, and the cousins—all dressed from church. Mom was serving dinner and when she turned around—there he was!

He remembered telling Billy later—"Wow, you should have seen her face. I guess I looked bad—'Ralph, the hippy'—

with all my dressed-up cousins. Mom hugged me when I gave her the Mother's Day card, and I said, 'You didn't think I'd forget you on Mother's Day?' She just cried and hugged me, and sat me down in her place at the table ... and what a dinner! I wanted to see the farm one more time."

> Go out there Dan
> Possess the land
> You move one step at the time
> We walk by faith
> And not by sight
> We move one step at the time.

It was getting dark and time to get back to the gang. He looked out again across the ocean, then rose and moved slowly across the rocks while the spray still blew in the wind. He touched the letter in his pocket. For a moment the wind swept the fog from his mind and he saw home, the farm, and his street, Bethel Spring Dale. From across the miles he heard her—that voice kept coming closer—"Ralph Jensen, in the name of Jesus, rise up and walk, rise up and walk. Come back to your Father's house. Rise up and walk. Rise up and walk."

He looked around. He was all alone—alone with the wind and the roll of the ocean. But he heard her, he knew he heard her! The voice followed him. "Rise up and walk—back to the Father's house."

14

Give Up the Prey

My dear Ralph,

Uncle Jack is coming August the first and Auntie Do rented a place at the beach August 8 to 16—so we can all take turns. Uncle Jack loves the ocean. We go to Atlantic Beach at Morehead City August 23 to 31.

Dan and Dad posted the land, checked state roads, and put up signs. Order in for Duke Power for a big light pole. Today they swing blade a clearing around the apple tree so Doris and I can pick apples.

Sunday, we visited the neighbors and sat on their porch and looked clear across Hanging Rock—absolutely terrific!

The old man looked like Grandpa Jensen, and talked about his wife, who died in 1967.

"We had 49 years," he told us. "Started out in the holler in a log cabin. Law—but she was purty, and smart, too! I grieved. Then one night the Lord let me see her—right thar, laying in the bed beside me—so purty and smiling. I just reached over to kiss her and

85

she looked at me, and she was done gone! But, oh Lord, she looked so happy and purty. Guess the Lord let me see her so I wouldn't grieve no more."

He wiped his eyes and said, "Gonna be nice to have folks in the valley. Used to have a path for a horse to ride. The last folks were evil, drinkin' folks—got killed in that holler. I'd check that well—no telling who or what be in that well. Mighty good to have Christian folks—gits so lonesome, just the birds, the pines in the wind. But I don't mind, cause I know she's happy. The Lord done showed me, cause I grieved so much. So purty!"

By that time I was grieving and just wanted to hug the grandpa. I said, "First chance we get, we'll have you come for supper." Boy, he lit up then.

Then we got scared, thinking of all the demons of violence down in our beautiful valley.

Duane [my nephew] said, "We'll just go down there and shout, 'Praise the Lord' and chase all the haunting spirits out. Then the whole community will see the change when Jesus moves in and the devil's crowd moves out." He is terrific—that kid!

Dan met another terrific neighbor—coming over to offer advice. There's another hundred acres joining Dan's backside and Auntie Do is heading out to see the man today. We are also checking on some adjoining the other side.

Whew! There is so much to do—but gradually we'll get at it. I guess we'll end up with a prayer meeting in the valley.

God bless you—but *write*, you stinker!

We love you,

Mom

Ralph took the letter and decided to go for a hike. There

were eleven boys living in a mansion, surrounded by stone fences, rolling fields, and gardens, but he needed to be alone. Why couldn't he just pull out and leave? No, he had bills to pay and these were his friends. At least he had work now and maybe he could make it and then go home—just to visit. He had to prove he could do it on his own. He had wrecked the car dad had given him and now he was fixing up an old van. He pulled out another letter. *Wonder why I save all Mom's letters? Oh, well!*

> Dear Ralph,
>
> Please drop your grandparents a note. They just returned from Norway. Grandpa is 82. I called them last night and they are so happy, and had walked to the shopping center and had ice cream. They said they love it there, but want to come to North Carolina. "Count us in," said mother.
>
> Uncle Jack and Dan left for Morehead and then will go to Wrightsville Beach in Wilmington on Sunday. Jan and Heather come Saturday, Jud comes August 15. Jud's parents come the 23rd of August.
>
> Hope you can make it then.
>
> Love you! Rite!!
>
> Mom

Man, oh, man, I sure would like to see Heather, such a cute baby! Wish I had some money so the guys could have a big fish supper tonight. Everyone was broke. The little money they made seemed to go for gas and repairs on old cars. He had bills up to his ears. What he wouldn't give to be free—really free—to go home and be on that farm and build a house and ride a horse. *Wouldn't you know, Dad bought Dan a horse. Dan gets everything! He even bought him a car.*

He kept walking and talking to the wind and the haunting reminder came: how Dad had bought him a car and how Mom had been furious! Dad even had given him a heavy leather, fur-lined jacket. Mom hadn't been too happy about that either—thought he should work for some things. Well he always did work, but the money went faster than he could make it. It really was a rotten world.

How come Jan and Dan were so good and he had to be the black sheep of the family? He felt as though chains held him in a world he didn't want to stay in. Was there no way out? *A bunch of guys in a big house! So what? That's not really a family. I want my own place, a wife, and kids. If only I could break free and do what I know is right.*

He stuffed the letters in his pocket. Those letters! Everyone read them—no secrets in this place! It was late and time to get supper—beans, maybe.

"Hey, Ralph," Billy yelled. "Just got back from the post office. Another sermon from your mom. Come on, you guys, Ralph's mom just sent another letter. Let's see what she says this time!"

> Dear Ralph,
>
>   I had a strong impression to send you $25. Get some good fish for all the gang. Just thought you might be hungry.
>
>   I love you,
>   Mother

"Wow—let's go! No beans tonight! Hey, Ralph, what's the other letter?"

"She sent a letter inside and said not to open it until I'm alone—so I guess we eat first!"

Within minutes frying pans were ready, vegetables peeled, and the boys waited for Ralph to return with the fish for supper. There was enough money for ice cream and cookies later. The coffeepot was perking on the stove. "Wonder what Ralph's mom wrote in that letter?" Billy mused. He, too, was haunted by letters from his mom.

It was late! Everyone had eaten and some had drifted off to their old habits that seemed unbreakable. Ralph sat alone in his room. He didn't want to read another letter—yet mom had sent the money for them. He knew she didn't have it. Reluctantly he opened the sealed envelope.

My dear Ralph,

Something strange happened to me while driving my car to work. I heard (not audibly) a silky voice—subtle and silky—say, "Give Ralph up. Let him go. Let him go. Let him go."

You don't know how many times I have become so weary and sick, watching you throw your life away in sin, that I have almost said, "I'm through. Ralph can go." No one had such love, such prayer and concern from the entire family and still refused to obey God.

I could see the devil laughing, "Give Ralph up—let him go. I want him because he can lead many my way."

Suddenly I could feel the Holy Spirit inside me making intercession with groanings that cannot be uttered or understood. I could feel the prayer go up through me to God.

Then I could sense an interpretation to what I was praying and I cried out, "In the name of Jesus, Ralph, rise up and walk. Walk in obedience to God's way and God will do His mighty acts." That is the same prayer I wrote before. God *is* speaking to you.

This A.M. the Lord showed me many things again when I determined to obey. This time I will fast and pray until you come through.

My fasting for you can only do certain things—prayer releases power to fight the enemy in this spiritual warfare, and to break the bonds of wickedness (Satan's hold on your affairs and thinking).

Isaiah 58: Fasting 1. breaks the bonds of wickedness; 2. looses the bands of the yoke (undoes the ties that keep the yoke on you).

Ralph, follow me closely. *You must break* the enslaving yoke. I can't do that. God can't do it. That enslaving yoke is *your will*. It hooks you to the world, that identity with the world. That is the shackle Satan uses to keep you yoked to him—*your will!* Jesus says, "Take My yoke and learn of Me." Jesus asks you—does not force you. Satan forces.

The key is "learn of Me." The reason you are in such conflict is that you have not broken the yoke that still enslaves you to Satan's identification.

I, too, am learning. I am learning, "Not by might, nor by power, but by My Spirit!" I am learning to die to desires (for creative writing??? for doing the things most women do—out to lunch and shopping and fun things). Every spare moment I'm in the Word—to keep an open heart to listen, to fast, pray, and walk alone that I might move in the Spirit—to lift you up before the throne, and to open my heart to you, to write (Mom's epistles), and share.

I get weary, Ralph, and sometimes feel the time is wasted. Lena keeps reminding me, "You done birthed him in the spirit, and he be coming out of that dark world into glorious light and he'll be naked, hungry, and yelling!"

That was last January and now it is August. Ralph, you are so loved. I love you so much, Ralph, and miss you. You have that certain something no one else in the family has.

Duane got a beautiful puppy and came to show us

and he was so excited he could scarcely talk. Everyone was too busy to pay attention and later someone said, "If Ralph had been here, he'd know how it feels to get something you've always wanted."

I turned to Doris and said, "Ralph has a feel for life. He responds to living things—a certain reverence for beauty. Oh, Do, I miss him."

Your aunt Doris is my prayer partner, with Lena. The Bible says, two or three—. We aren't taking any chances. We are three!

Love,
Mother

P.S. I hope you all had a good dinner. I love all the boys in your house, and pray for them.

Mom

Ralph took off to his place of retreat—the rocky coast, where the ocean's roar mingles with the sound of the seagulls. Night was coming on, but he sat, high on the rocks, looking out over the dark waters. Tormented by regret, filled with fear, haunted by a demonic world of fantasy, he longed for home and righteousness. He wanted the best of both worlds; sooner or later he would have to choose. That yoke! He was strangled, chained, and held in torment. *How did Mom know? Does she really hear from God?* His thoughts ran together. He wanted to run, but where?

Then it came again—across the wind—"Rise up and walk, back to your father's house. Everything you ever longed for is right back where you left it. Rise up and walk! Rise up and walk!"

Later, much later, he reached for the telephone. This time he dialed home. He heard it ringing.

Back in Greensboro, I missed Lena during the summer months when the college infirmary was closed. I missed the cup of coffee and the crust of bread, but most of all I missed her singing and constant reminder, "Don't you be letting no coonching spirits of doubt and unbelief come in this kitchen."

With my open Bible before me I sat in my own kitchen watching the ducks and geese glide in formation across the quiet lake. Coffee cup in hand, I nibbled on my crust of bread and remembered the phone call to Lena the night before.

"Oh, Lena, it's been so long, but I know the answer is coming. I sense a great spiritual warfare. Besides, I miss you."

"You talks about a battle, child. I be in one where I work this summer. I'm in a house with sickness and rebellious children, and I just pray and sing all day. I know Jesus is right with me to help that family.

"Sister Jensen, it seems to be that God's children be the ones to take care of the devil's crowd."

"It's been a long, hard summer, Lena, and after weeks of nursing my friend Lydia, she died quietly in my arms. I kept my promise to her, that I would take care of her at home. I stayed and helped the family with all the arrangements.

"Janice and Heather are coming and we are all making plans to go to Morehead City for a good vacation of fishing and swimming. And we've been very busy on the farm. It seems that all the pressures come at once. During all this, we were fasting and praying and still no answer! Don't worry, I'm not giving up. 'Unclog the channel! Keep believing and you'll be seeing.' I'm getting to sound more like you every day, Lena. O.K., we agree together: In the name of Jesus, Ralph, rise up and walk."

I poured another cup of coffee and thanked God for a new day. And decided that, like Lena would say, "No devil gonna take it from me." I turned to face the day the Lord had made.

Dan and Harold had gone to the airport to meet Janice and Heather.

Before I knew it, the car pulled into the driveway and the sounds of a home filled the house. Heather, ten months old, held us all her willing captives. Dan and Jan talked about the beach and Harold dragged out old suitcases.

The round kitchen table found us all talking about Ralph. Heather banged her spoon on the new highchair and laughed her approval. *How Ralph used to love this*, I thought. *Everyone around the table, laughing and talking.*

"Enough talk, Dan, let's get this fishing gear together. You and Jan can talk all the way to the beach." Harold urged us on and the packing began in earnest. The hours flew. Before we knew it we were ready to leave. Harold was heading out to the car.

That's when the phone rang! I answered, and a familiar voice from across the miles said, "Mama, I want to come home!"

15

The Purple Van

Harold sat on the porch, waiting. Jan wrapped her arms around her father, "I'm sorry, Daddy. He should have been here by now. Maybe the pull was too great, once he got the money you sent him."

"He'll come!"

"Dad, why don't you come with us fishing? Help pass the time."

"Thanks, Dan, but I'll wait right here. I can watch the cars come over the bridge."

"But, Dad, you've been sitting there for three days."

"He'll come! I know he'll come!"

The spacious summer home looked over the ocean. Dan, Jud, and his father, Robert Carlberg, headed for the boat, fishing gear in hand. Jan was getting ready for a swim. Helen Carlberg, Jud's mother, was in the kitchen serving French toast for breakfast. It was a beautiful day!

In my mind, I could hear Lena's voice, "God give us a brand-new day, and no devil going to take it away. Don't let those coonching spirits of doubt and unbelief come sneaking in."

Ralph's room was ready, new sheets on the bed, and a gentle breeze blowing through the soft curtains.

I felt the agony and ecstasy raging within me—a battle between doubt and hope.

Harold sat on the porch remembering the phone call of a few days ago: "Mama, I want to come home." He had been packing the car when I called to him, "It's Ralph." Then Harold heard the same words I had heard: "Daddy, I want to come home!"

"Ralph, I want you home more than anything else. We are leaving for Morehead, with all the fishing gear, so meet us at Charlie's place. You'll probably catch all the big ones."

"Dad, I can't come home. I'm broke."

"How much do you need? I'll send money special delivery. Just take care of your bills and head for Morehead."

"I'll pay you back, Dad—and thanks."

"Don't even think of any payback! God bless you, Ralph, and have a safe trip. Remember, we love you."

At Morehead, Harold decided not to go fishing. Instead he sat on the porch. "He'll come. I know he'll come, and I'll be right here, waiting."

The cars moved slowly over the bridge and with them relentlessly rolled the memories of the irreparable past. I had read somewhere that God is the God of our yesterdays. He allows us the memory of them so we can turn the past into a ministry for the future.

How often we had wondered what we could or should have done differently. Who was to blame? The family? The church? Society?

We shared that past: the struggle to obtain an education; the call to the pastoral ministry; the idealistic devotion to evangelical causes, the love for home and family; and, above all, our dedication to Christ.

Our children had always been a part of our lives, in work or recreation. They had always been with us—trips, picnics, mountains, beaches. Why would one stray so far from us?

I wondered how much effect one nightmarish experience could have on a young child. Was Harold remembering also? It was a long time ago.

Ralph was two years old when Harold had gone into a rural area with a passionate abandonment to obey God and pastor the rich and poor, black and white.

But cultural misunderstanding, ignorance, and fear of change brought battle-line hostilities. The way of tradition seemed to war against the grace of God to change people's hearts. Harold chose to leave quietly rather than allow the ministry to be a battlefield. Four-year-old Ralph chose to smash his tiny clenched fist into the face of a man who had cursed his father.

"That's not the way we do it, Ralph," Harold had said. Jan and Dan were older and understood. *Could the seed of rebellion have found fertile soil in this one so young?* I wondered.

Harold later chose to travel in church promotional work, so he was on the road much of the time during Ralph's teen years. Jan married and Dan went away to school. I was working as a nurse. The unique closeness we enjoyed with our young children was now divided into special times, like holidays and vacations. *Perhaps the youngest felt the changing times more than the rest of us did,* I wondered. Yet, I also knew that into each heart is given the measure of faith to believe—and the free will to choose. We all learn from the past, and no situation is perfect. We have a sovereign God who is able to do more than we can ask or think. Lena would say, "This be a trusting time."

Somehow I knew that rejection, bitterness and unforgiveness had to be dealt with—even in the very young. My prayer was that our family would allow God's love to flow through us in the days to come.

I read in my journal, "One of the greatest strains in life is waiting for God." I also wondered how often we break the heart of God while He waits for us. "This be a waiting time." Finally, I knew Ralph would come. And Harold would be waiting, watching the cars move over the bridge.

Then he saw it!

A purple van moved slowly in the traffic and pulled into the driveway of the beach house. Within seconds, Harold gathered his youngest son in his arms, and then we were all hugging him at once.

The haunted eyes looked through us. Immediately, I recognized the unhealthy yellow pallor of his skin. Like a tortured prisoner, he had managed to escape. I knew the real journey home had just begun. Fleeting words ran across my mind, *I have miles to go before I sleep.* "Oh, Lena, Lena," I cried to myself, "I thought the battle was over, but it is just beginning. God help us!"

Outwardly I talked about swimming and fishing, and suggested that we all have breakfast first. After a good sleep, he could tell us about his trip.

"Helen, here we are, and here is Ralph." Turning from the stove, Jud's mother covered the horror in her eyes with her quiet dignity. The tall young man was not the Ralph she remembered, but she said gently, "Ralph, how nice to see you. Please sit down and here is some French toast."

Ralph ate hungrily. Heather climbed on his lap to pull his beard and then settled herself there. She had a friend.

After a warm shower, he fell exhausted into a clean bed. I pulled the sheet to tuck him in, and I kissed my youngest son goodnight. He was asleep.

We cleaned the van and took the soiled clothes to the laundry. When he awakened from several hours of refreshing sleep, he had clean clothes—and an appointment at the barbershop.

The following days were filled with sunshine, swimming, fishing, and eating. Refreshing sleep, good food, and relaxing hours with the family brought a measure of healing to his weary mind and body.

Too soon it was time to leave. Lena and I had to open the infirmary for a new school year. Jan and Jud had to return to Michigan State University. Dr. and Mrs. Carlberg were returning to their ministry, Brooklyn Baptist Temple. Everyone was leaving at a different time. Ralph was to follow us home in his van.

A few days later Lena and I were back in the kitchen to dedicate another school year to the Lord. Ralph, too, came to sit at the table for a cup of coffee and a crust of bread.

"Lord have mercy, child, Lena need to be cooking you some pinto beans and cornbread. I just stomps on them coonching spirits that want to send you back to that 'Chusetts' place. What those folks know about feeding a southern boy? What they know about big fat biscuits with country ham, red-eye gravy, and grits? They never heard tell of pot licker and chittling bread. You right where you belong—where we be putting some meat on your bones. That Satum don't give up easy, but I told that devil to go."

"Lena, you won't believe what happened to me when I left the guys in Massachusetts. My friend, Billy Welker, came home to Greensboro, and I guess I'll be seeing him. We've been friends since second grade. My friends in Massachusetts couldn't believe I was leaving, and neither could I. I still don't know how I got here. Anyhow, Dad sent the money and I paid up my bills—school and car repairs—and then gave a guy a ride to Virginia Beach. That was O.K., because I had someone to talk to. When I was alone though, it was like an army of demons in my van, telling me to go back. Sometimes I thought I would lose my mind, and I forgot where I was. My van wanted to turn around—almost like someone else driving it. I had to scream out loud to shut out the voices telling me to turn around."

"Oh, child, that be when your mama and I be praying. 'Lord Jesus, send the angels to bring that boy home.'"

"When I got to Morehead, Lena, you'll never guess what happened! Two guys in front of my van, right on the street, were flipped out on drugs and having a bad trip. I got out of my van to help them and talk them down. By that time I couldn't even remember where Charlie's big house was. I fell asleep in the van, and when the police woke me up I was right across the highway from Charlie's ... where Dad told me to come. It was all so weird. When I pulled up in the driveway—there was Dad. He had been sitting on the porch three days—and wouldn't leave. All the time the devil was telling me he didn't care."

"He did more than wait, child, he prayed. That be how that van couldn't turn around. The angels be having a big war with the devil's crowd. God won! Glory to Jesus! Hallelujah! Praise the Lord!"

"Lena, you should have seen me in that barbershop in Morehead. I had an audience, inside and outside. The barber was so mad he cussed me the whole time he cut my hair. He even broke his clippers!

"I figured I had hurt Mom enough and decided to get that long hair off. But I wouldn't let that barber touch my beard. I still belong to my family in Massachusetts—I think."

"God be looking on the heart, child, and one day you be set free. It's the heart needs changing—not the hair, but I must say you looks good with the long hair off."

Ralph came and went, quietly battling a tortured warfare alone.

"Victory coming, Sister Jensen. Just don't be organizing ways for God to do His work. This be our waiting time. God sending out those angels behind the bushes to confuse the enemy that try to send our boy back to that 'Chusetts place."

The days flew by, filled with the activity of a new school year—reports, physicals, sick call, returning students, and students who stopped by to say hello. New students came, timidly asking, "We've heard about Lena. Is she here?" She was!

Ralph enjoyed his days at the farm, swinging an ax, clearing land, or taking long hikes through the woods.

Life goes on, somehow. Dan was busy teaching school in the mountains, and Jan and Jud were busy in Michigan. Harold was traveling. Lena and I clung to the "believing is seeing." She wouldn't let me doubt.

The purple van stayed!!

16

The Guest Room

It was the second week in September and Greensboro College classes were in full swing. Warm, hazy days left over from summer made outdoor activity more desirable than books and libraries. The colds and sore throats would come later, but now everyone seemed well.

Lena and I sat at our table for early morning coffee.

"We've come to the end of another week, Nurse, and Ralph still with us. One of these days he'll find a job and that restless spirit be gone. We still believing."

"When I get home today, Lena, I have to get the guest room ready. The banquet speaker for the Business Men's Organization is coming from New Jersey. He'll be our guest for the weekend. That room is seldom empty."

"I remember how we surprised Jan when she came home from Wheaton College. She walked into her new room—all pink and white, with white organdy ruffled curtains and a pink shag rug. How she loved that room! But when she married Jud I decided to make it look more like a guest room—soft gold and moss green. It's a restful room.

"Remember last year when Moa and Becky stayed there?"

"Too bad you didn't keep a guest book, so many folks coming and going. Some folks be mighty famous these days."

"I was too busy to remember the guest book. I remember when Pat Robertson was a guest. He was the speaker at the King Cotton Hotel and even went swimming with Ralph at the Hamilton Lakes Pool, but Ralph can't remember. Our friend, Harold Bredesen, a world traveler, slept in that room. Evelio Perez, from Mexico, came often and how we loved to hear him play the guitar and sing, 'His loving kindness is better than life.' You are right, Lena, I should have kept a guest book, because I can't remember all the wonderful people who stayed in that room—missionaries and evangelists from all around the world. The one I can never forget is Steve Bezuidenhaut from South Africa. He was a young handsome dynamo, one of Ralph's favorites, during high-school days. Steve loved cars and motorcycles, and he and Ralph even went camping together. Since Steve had been such a rebel himself he certainly could identify with Ralph. He won Ralph's respect because, 'He enjoys living, Mom, and doesn't preach at you.'"

"How many folks been praying for that boy in that room— all those preachers and missionaries, and the churches in town? Seems like the Lord kept an army of angels around that child."

"Oh, Lena, I wrote everyone—seems like I had everyone praying. One time Steve Bezuidenhaut said, 'O Lord, save that Ralph. I'm tired of praying for him.'"

"What happens to folks who have no one to pray for them?"

Lena looked out the window and called out the names of the students on their way to the dining room. "Just can't stop praying till Jesus comes."

"That's not all, Lena, just look at my family—besides Harold, Jan, Jud, and Dan. My parents in Brooklyn never forget to pray, my sister Grace, my brother Gordon. Doris in

Winston-Salem comes in often to pray with me. My sister Joyce, and Howard, in Arkansas, and Jeanelle in Florida. Uncle Jack in Arkansas prays for everyone in the family by name."

"Oh, thank You, Jesus, all those prayers coming up before You! All this big family, all these churches and preachers. That room filled with the prayers of Your people, Jesus. We be seeing the believing soon. Bless the man coming to speak, and thank You for taking care of our boy. You alone can set him free."

Lena was singing and getting her beat. We were about to have church before the day's activity got into full gear.

The hours flew by and before we knew it the week had come to a close and the infirmary was locked for the weekend.

"I'll see you at the meeting tomorrow night—and don't be organizing too much." Lena's laughter rang out as she crossed the campus to catch her bus for home.

I eased my car over the bridge of the lake, and stopped long enough to watch the geese and ducks glide in formation over the water. The birds and squirrels seemed to be enjoying the last lazy summer days. I headed for my driveway and the duties ahead.

My garden was bursting with red and gold mums, so I picked a basketful for the house. I placed a small vase of golden flowers in the guest room. The Bible, magazines, and books on the night table made the finishing touches complete. Tomorrow morning I would bake cookies and pecan rolls and get a ham for Sunday dinner. I never knew how many we would have after church, so I stayed prepared. Ralph was gone for the day, still so very restless.

When Saturday morning dawned, soft and warm, I found my favorite spot by the window, overlooking the lake. With my coffee cup in hand I read my verse again. The verse I had claimed for nine months was Isaiah 49:25: "But thus saith the

Lord, Even the captives of the mighty shall be taken away, and the prey of the terrible shall be delivered: for I will contend with him that contendeth with thee, and I will save thy children."

I thanked God for a brand-new day.

I set the dough for rolls and started the baking and food preparations. My kitchen was alive with joy and expectancy. Surely Ralph would go with us to the meeting to hear our guest, Earl Prickett.

I prayed and believed while I rolled out pecan rolls and took cookies out of the oven. The table was set for lunch and I wondered why Harold and Dan, who had gone to the airport, were late in bringing our guest home.

Later, when I was taking the rolls out of the oven, I heard them laughing and talking out in the driveway.

White hair framed a face of pure joy, while Earl's blue eyes had the mischievous look of a boy with a cookie jar. With a bear hug and a shout of "Praise the Lord," he told me they had gone to the farm.

"Oh, no wonder," I laughed, "might have known Dan had to take you to Shalom."

Within moments we were around the table, where Earl shared story after story, recounting events from his world travels.

How I wished Ralph were here—but he seemed to know when to be gone. I knew Ralph would love this man with his warm down-to-earth humor. I prayed he'd come home in time for the banquet meeting at 7 P.M.

Everyone had time to rest before the meeting. I waited!

The banquet room was packed with a happy crowd which represented many denominations. The music was triumphant. Bob Adams played one of his own compositions on the clarinet, and Dorothy Weymann, as always, made the piano pour forth music. Cy Moffit led the singing, and the joy of the Lord filled the place. Lena was having church at our table.

When Earl stood up to speak, his message was, "If you can believe, you'll see the glory of the Lord." Lena gave me a knowing look—"like I be telling you, the believing comes before the seeing." I watched the door, but Ralph didn't come.

Later, much later, when the house was still, I watched the cars coming around the lake. Fear clutched at me, *Maybe he's gone again.* Then I saw the purple van coming slowly over the bridge. I slipped quietly to bed, thanking God, Ralph was still here.

In the guest room rested one of God's faithful servants—and one more prayer had winged its way to the throne.

Faith was hearing the approaching footsteps of God's salvation.

17

The Broken Joe

"Lena, you wouldn't believe the stories that man told!"

Ralph stretched his long legs beside the kitchen table while Lena poured a cup of coffee.

"I do more believing than doubting—so I be listening, child."

"Remember Billy Welker?"

"Don't tell me what that child be up to. Seems to me you two been in trouble since second grade." Lena's hearty laugh made talking easy.

"Well, we haven't laughed so hard in years. I invited Billy home for Sunday dinner. Mom's used to Billy coming any old time. And that Earl Prickett told so many stories about people from all over the world. Lena, he's not a preacher—dresses real sharp, and can he tell the jokes! He says a lot, but doesn't preach. If I had known he was that sharp, maybe I wouldn't have stayed away on Saturday. I knew Mom was planning on dragging me to that meeting—but more sermons I didn't need. After all, I've heard sermons all my life. I could even preach a few myself. But, Lena, this guy was so happy, Billy and I didn't want to leave. But they were talking about a meeting at Daltons' in High Point, so we decided to be long gone."

"Ralph, Earl was a very sick man, about to die from sin and drinking and disease. He lost everything he had. He was a mighty sad man. Then Jesus found him and set him free and healed him. The joy he be having so much of is the joy of the Lord. Now he's telling the world about Jesus. Thank You Jesus—for setting us free! The ones that be chained so long be the ones who shout the most when they gets free."

"Yeah, Lena, I know about chains. Sometimes I feel those chains pulling me back to Massachusetts and my old friends. I used to pace the roads and walks. I paced the rocky shore by the ocean. I couldn't just take a walk. I had to go-go-go—any place, just be moving."

"That be a restless spirit. That Satum put on you. I hates that Satum! He torments the young more now than he ever do before—even little children. I watch them in the grocery store—restless and rebellious, even riding around in the grocery cart. Children's didn't used to be so restless."

"Lena, I've always been restless. I resented the people who had been so cruel to my father. I never wanted to be like them—and they were good Christians! I resented Christians—not my folks—but I thought all the rest were hypocrites and I was out to get even.

"That's why I didn't get along at Gordon. Now I realize how hard Dean Gross and others—even the cook—tried to help me. There are some things I won't forget. Dan and Jan aren't like me. They can forgive and forget, but I just think about the injustice done by some Christians."

"Now Ralph boy, I know something about not being treated fair. Some folks say they be Christians—but not act like Christians. Aren't you forgetting about _all_ the Christians you know? Them good ones? You see so much bad you be blind to the good. When I was very young I had a knowing about folks not fair to Jesus, so I said, 'Lena, you not better than Jesus. If He be your friend, for what you worry about other folks, black or white?' Someday my Jesus makes everything fair and right. I can wait! I be used to waiting! Good things coming, Ralph. You best be learning about waiting. That's why you be home now. Pretty strong rope holding you here. You done got the promise in that letter your mama wrote, that letter about 'Rise up and walk.' Your mama learned to wait.

"By the way child, how did you break that toe? It looks bad—all big and purple. You best get some ice on that foot and put it up on a big pillow. You stay home and don't go driving none. Keep that foot up, hear?"

"Oh, Lena, you won't believe how that happened! I went to Charlotte Saturday—just to get away from that meeting. You know something? It's hard to be around a crowd of happy people when you are so miserable. I figured the best thing for me was either to join them or get far away. You can't stay in the middle with that crowd. Same thing at the Masons' prayer meeting next Tuesday night. Boy oh boy, Lena, you better believe I'll be long gone that Tuesday night meeting. Wow!

"Anyhow, back to Charlotte...and this girl! Boy—the messes I get into! Almost married a little Russian atheist in Massachusetts. I thought I could convert her. How's that for thinking, Lena? Then there was that cute little Scandinavian blond—me, 6' 5" and she was 4' 5". Wow! What a pair we made! She wore my T-shirt for a dress. Oh brother, I almost— oh well, forget it. Then Mom's letter. That blew me. Here I was searching and searching and Mom writes, 'Everything you longed for is here where you left it.' Lena, I couldn't get away from it. So, naturally, when I met this girl in Charlotte, I figured she might be the one.

"We were sitting in the van, and I was really thinking about marrying her. My head was a muddle! I thought if I get married and someone really belonged to me I wouldn't be so restless. You know, Lena, I actually felt the chains pulling me back to Massachusetts. Another strange thing though, I also felt a rope tying me to home. What a crazy world!"

"Oh, child, you are feeling the rope of love. That rope be there when you a little iddy baby. God somehow had it figured out that we be tied to our mama so we never be forgetting where we gets our life. Sometimes the papas don't be at the birthings, but there be no birthing without the mama. There be no life without God. Life comes from God and whatever come from God—well, that be good. All the bad come from Satum. He the one sending all them coonching spirits to be dragging you away from your family."

Lena stomped her foot and swept the kitchen furiously with her broom. "I sweep that Satum out this kitchen. Swoosh!" Ralph chuckled at her vehemence.

"Don't you be laughing, boy. When you ever get mad enough at that Satum and stomp on him, then that devil leave you for sure. Trouble be we put up with him and don't resist. The Bible says, 'Resist the devil, and he will flee from you.' The devil sends a coonching spirit and whispers, 'That be not so.' He is a liar, who only wants to kill or destroy everyone that be birthed. He brings confusion to everything we do. One thing I know for sure, and that is, greater is Jesus in me than that devil trying to coonch on me. Oh, thank You Jesus! God is greater!

"Now we get back to the birthing. God sets us in families, the Bible says. That's so we not be forgetting where life comes from. Terrible sin not to honor your father and mother. God never said, 'Honor them if they be perfect.' Some folks are plumb bad. It's not the bad you honor, it's the giver of life—that cord that be tied to your mama. If the folks that done birthed a child be bad, that child been given life so he can grow up and choose. How you choose good if you not be birthed? Even in bad families God sends His love some way so a child can choose. That's why we must live lives that the others can study about. When that birthed child grow up he can see somebody good and want to be good. I know there be good and bad mamas and papas, but they give life. Whatever comes from God—that be good.

"Now Lena got to preaching again—and we plumb got away from that Charlotte girl. You do have a way with girls. Oh, I can figure out that cause you sure got a way with your mama—and Lena. Sometimes I gets the feeling your mama loves her youngest the best. Now don't you be telling Jan and Dan that."

"Oh come on, Lena, you know Mom and Dad think Jan and Dan are perfect. Maybe that's why I stayed away. Nothing I did was right. They were always so good. Maybe that's why I almost married girls so different from Jan. I guess I never thought I was good enough for a girl like my sister. Now you take Dan—no one is good enough for him. He really is a terrific brother, even if he makes me feel inferior. O.K.—now as to that girl! Oh, Lena, you won't believe what happened."

"Try me—I pretty believing!" Lena's laughter rang out and, with his defenses down, Ralph rambled on with perfect ease. *It was so easy to talk to Lena,* he thought. She never had that hurt, condemning look. Something about Lena almost made him believe life could be better. She made him feel strong on the inside. Maybe that's why the kids on campus came to her kitchen—the one place they felt comfortable. It didn't seem to matter to her whether a person was white or black. Most of us feel baffled by the complexity of life. Lena made life seem simple—maybe like it used to be. Oh, how he wished life were simple. He remembered the anger of some church people because his Dad had helped the poor people— black and white. The Christians had called him a communist. When he was in kindergarten, Ralph's teacher asked why he drew farms and horses. He said he wanted to be where everyone loved us—and a farm didn't have people. Horses and dogs don't get angry at people. Some church people stay mad at everybody. He hated being a preacher's kid.

Lena quietly put toast in the oven and made another pot of coffee. "Your head going round and round, Ralph boy. You be going back too much and you remembering the bad and forgetting the good. You know why that be? That be because Satum—oh I hate that Satum—he got no future. He only got the past to work on, so he torments folks with the past—all the bad past—so folks be forgetting what they supposed to remember, and that be the good traditions and who taught them, like Paul told Timothy. God holds today. The Bible says, 'Now is the day of salvation.'[1] The Bible says, 'Forget the things of the past and press forward.'[2] Jesus blots out the sin and buries it in the ocean. Thank You, Jesus! Now you never got to that girl."

They laughed together. It was good to laugh and talk. "That's me all right, wandering in the wilderness. It was like this—this girl and I were in the van, and I wanted to talk to her about getting married, but she said, 'I don't know what's wrong, but I feel a wall between us.' And there was. Every time I tried to get close to her there was this wall. I turned on the radio, and it blared, 'This is Scott Ross coming to you in the name of the Lord Jesus Christ.' Just like that, I knew! We were definitely not for each other! But when I took her back to her dorm, Lena, my mind was so preoccupied I didn't watch where I was going, and I stepped off the sidewalk crooked—and broke my toe!"

"Well, child, maybe that one time you gave Satum one big kick—and he gave you a stomping on the toe. He getting mad, cause his time with you be getting short. Glory! Hallelujah to Jesus! It be working for good!

"Now you best get that toe tended to, and do what Lena say: no driving that van, and put that toe up!"

With a hug she sent him on his way. Lena watched the van pull out of the driveway. Standing by the window she quietly called out his name.

When the day came to an end I watched Lena close the kitchen door and walk across the campus to catch her bus for home. She was singing:

> We walk by faith
> And not by sight
> We move one step at the time.

18

The Phone Call

"Lena, Lena, guess what happened last night?" As soon as I walked into the infirmary the next morning, I wanted to talk to Lena.

"Come sit down. Got the oven toast ready and a pot of coffee. We talks better when we get that crust of bread. Today we have some homemade strawberry jam. This kitchen better than any T.V. show. Every day something new happen. God's people have a good time—even when praying for folks. We just keep the rejoicing heart and keep expecting miracles. No dragging, lonesome days for God's children—too much to do."

"The infirmary was so busy yesterday—the Monday blues, I guess—that I didn't get to tell you about Sunday night. Besides Ralph was in a talking mood—so I stayed clear."

"That boy coming—too much praying done for him not to."

"I know, Lena, but it's so hard to wait. He seems so close, and then he takes off. Running away from God isn't easy, and watching him struggle isn't easy for me either. I feel so helpless."

"Best way to feel, then we know only God can do it. Without Him we can do nothing. That I be knowing!"

"Sunday night, my friend Frances Dalton invited many influential guests to her beautiful home to meet Earl Prickett. People were free to ask questions, and since Earl is a successful businessman himself, he can respond to questions from other leading businessmen. Dan drove Earl to High Point, and, of course, Ralph disappeared so he wouldn't get roped into going."

"That's my child," Lena laughed. "He blows in and out like the wind. One day he stop running."

"It was a beautiful evening and when everyone was leaving, Frances said, 'There is someone we need to pray for, and it seems to be an urgent need. Don't go yet, let us stop long enough to ask God.'

"All of a sudden Dan spoke up, 'It's my brother, Ralph. I'll sit in proxy for him, and let's pray for my brother.'

"Within moments Dan was sitting on a chair and the Christian businessmen were gathered around him. Laying their hands on him, they prayed for Ralph. Together they bound the hindrances of the enemy and loosed the convicting power of the Holy Spirit to move in Ralph's heart. 'Be set free, in Jesus' name!'

"One man spoke up and said these words, 'A servant of the Lord is coming to minister to Ralph, and great will be the deliverance, and the deliverance of many.' Then everyone started to praise the Lord for answered prayer—before the answer was known."

"See, what I be saying all along—the believing come before the seeing."

"Of course, you know me, Lena, right away I said to Earl, 'You must be the man. Ralph enjoys you so much. You can't leave on that plane tomorrow. You just have to stay!'

"Very gently, he said, 'No, Margaret, I'm not the man, but trust God to do it His way. Don't try to figure it out. God will do it, and then you will always know God did it. Don't be overly anxious. But with prayer and thanksgiving let God do it.'

"Oh, Lena, Evelio used to say that to me over and over. 'Be anxious for nothing, Margaret—God will do it.' "

"Oh, child, we unclog the channel nine months ago, and been praising God ever since. Can't let no coonching spirits of doubt and unbelief be stirring up an anxious spirit. I told you, our child be birthed—crying, naked, and hungry. We be there to feed and clothe him. Thank You, Jesus!"

"Lena, I'm so excited, I can hardly tell you the rest of the story. Earl left on the plane, and Doris came for supper last night. We were eating on the porch, and, after supper, Ralph went upstairs to put his foot up. Dan, Harold, Doris, and I were enjoying the cool breeze on the porch when the phone rang.

"It was Steve Bezuidenhaut! I thought he was in South Africa, but he was conducting a meeting in Little Rock, Arkansas. In his crisp British accent he said, 'I don't understand it, but my plans have been changed. I was going to Kentucky, but the Lord spoke to me and said, "Go to Greensboro, to the Masons' prayer meeting." I really didn't want to change my plans, but God seemed to insist I go now. It seems urgent, somehow. Please call the Masons and tell them I'll be there. I must obey God.' "

"Praise the Lord, still some folks willing to listen to God. Not many be believing God speaks to people today, but why He not speak today when He told Paul and Peter what to do? Just folks not hearing."

"You should have seen us on that porch! We were just rejoicing—and all that time Ralph was upstairs with his sore toe up on a pillow listening to his radio. He had no idea what was going on downstairs."

"Oh, glory! Don't God's children have a good time? Why some church folks so sad and stiff-like I'll never be knowing.

All the time the Bible be telling folks to rejoice always, and that be good and bad times. That way you keeps your heart ready to listen and ready to receive. God be trying to give good things to His children and they be so stirred up with anxious fears they can't hear nothing God telling them. I don't tell too many folks about the day the Lord gave me a knowing not to buy that newspaper. I heard plumb sure in my heart, 'I have something to show you in My Word—no time for the paper today.' I had that piece of money in my hand, but when I gets a knowing I best be believing it. That be the day we unclog the channel and we been believing ever since. The seeing is about to come! Praise the Lord. Now be careful, walk soft-like and don't say much. Keep quiet and you'll be hearing what God tell you to do. God don't change. He be telling Moses, and He told Esther, and He told Ruth to sleep by that Boaz man. Lord have mercy, how about that for telling? I wish the Lord find me a Boaz man. I sure be listening if He tell me to sleep by him."

Lena's laughter filled the kitchen and we both felt the tension leave and the joy of peace fill the kitchen. Somehow I had an idea the angels in heaven must love Lena. She was always good for a laugh.

"Oh, Lena, I love you!"

Her black arms engulfed me and she added, "He's coming home, child, our boy be coming home. Keep a listening heart and you'll be hearing what to do next."

And so it came to pass that on my way home I met some of Ralph's old buddies. It was then I had a knowing.

"An old friend of Ralph's is coming to a meeting tonight at the Masons'. There will be lots of music, guitars, and a house full of young people. I'm going home now to bake a cherry pie and prepare Ralph's favorite meal. I'm sure Ralph would love to have you eat supper with us. How about it?"

"You mean Ralph has a preacher friend?"

"Oh, yes, Steve is quite a guy. They went camping together."

"Ralph camping with a preacher? This ought to be good! We got nothing to do—and we're starved. O.K. It's a deal! And—thanks!"

I watched them shuffle along aimlessly and wondered if they would come. But I knew they were hungry—and broke! Fay Turner, one of my favorite students, was also coming for supper. This really ought to be good! Now how to get Ralph to that meeting?

When I arrived home I flew into action—meatballs, gravy, mashed potatoes—and the cherry pie. When Fay came early we set the table as though for honored guests. Flowers and candles, china and silver. I was so excited I could hardly think. I just kept praying.

When Ralph came downstairs, limping with his sore toe, Fay rolled her blue eyes and in her honeyed southern drawl expressed her concern. And she told him some old friends were coming to hear Steve at the Masons'—after supper.

They came! Laughing and talking around the table, with Fay to tease, the boys ate hungrily and told their old jokes. I filled the dishes in the kitchen and Fay served. Relaxing over cherry pie and coffee, the boys were in a jovial mood. While Fay entertained them, I cleared the table and washed the dishes. Too excited to eat, I sipped a cup of coffee and wondered how we'd get Ralph to the meeting.

"Don't be anxious, and don't be organizing!" I could hear Lena's voice, "Let God do it!"

When it was time to leave, I heard Fay's soft southern drawl, "Oh, Ralphie, I don't know how to get to the Masons and we all want to hear Steve. So come with me in my car—since you can't drive the van. The others will follow."

I watched Fay take Ralph's hand and look up at him with those blue eyes and long eyelashes. The next thing I saw was

Ralph easing his long legs into Fay's car—heading for the prayer meeting. The others followed. I brought up the rear.

It was Tuesday night—7 P.M., September 15, 1970.

19

Rise Up and Walk

The sun had not yet risen when I opened the infirmary door, and then I saw Lena coming across the campus carrying a heavily loaded shopping bag. Her song rang out in the early morning, "Praise God, from whom all blessings flow; Praise Him all creatures here below."

"Glory hallelujah—my child been birthed!"

"But Lena, how did you know? You weren't there and it was so late. I couldn't call you at 4 A.M.!"

"The Lord woke me up and said, 'Lena, your child been birthed.' I just got out of bed and started praising my Jesus. He told me some other things, but first you tell me everything."

"What's in that bag, Lena?"

"That bag come later—now I hear about my boy."

"Oh, Lena, you should have seen those boys eat—and Ralph's eyes followed Fay like a lamb. If his toe hadn't been so sore he probably would have sneaked out the back door to his van. But there he was, in the Masons' prayer meeting in a corner with his long legs stretched out.

"The guitars were playing and you could hear the music a block away—organ, piano, clarinet, violin, and guitars. Oh, it was wonderful! You could tell the boys—and Ralph—were really impressed with such a crowd, sitting on the floor, stairs, kitchen, and hall—filling every corner! Dan was there, my sister Doris, Frances Dalton from High Point, and lots of friends who had been praying for years. I was squeezed into a corner.

"All of a sudden the door opened and in walked Steve Bezuidenhaut. His blond curly hair framed a determined face, and his clear blue eyes looked right through the crowd. With his crisp British accent, he called out, 'Hallelujah! Praise the Lord!' With the clear voice of authority he announced, 'I have a message from the Lord! Ye must be born again!'[1]

"*Oh no, I groaned to myself. That's all these kids have ever heard from preachers. I expected Steve to come like Elijah, with fire from heaven—dramatic and earth shaking.*"

Lena rolled her eyes in mock dismay and shook her finger. I continued about Steve.

" 'Tonight I'll tell you what happened to me when God touched me.'

"For the next thirty minutes he held those hundred people spellbound. He recounted his youthful life of rebellion—wine, women, and song. He described his last desperate night, sitting in an empty nightclub saying, 'I've done it all. Now what?'

" 'God came to me with the words I had heard all my life from my preacher father, "You must be born again." That night I surrendered my will, and gave my life to Jesus. He delivered me from darkness into his glorious light. Someone here needs a touch from God.'

"Oh Lena, you should have been there! At that moment Steve saw Ralph's big toe sticking out, and with his wonderful sense of humor he smiled, 'Looks like this somebody needs a touch from God. Come up here!'

"Ralph stood there, Lena, all six feet five inches of him.

"Steve said, 'Buddy, what's your name?' "

"Lena, those hollow eyes looked into Steve's bright eyes and in such a plaintive voice Ralph said, 'Oh, Steve, don't you even know me?'

"I cried, Lena.

"Steve's blue eyes pierced through Ralph and Steve cried, 'My God—it's Ralph!'

"That room full of people called out, 'It's Ralph. It's the Jensen boy! The one we've been praying for.' Some were weeping, others rejoicing. No one had recognized him.

"Steve continued in that commanding voice, 'Ralph Jensen, you have been running long enough. You need more than your toe healed. You need deliverance from the enemy. You need to be born again. Do you want to be free?'

"Ralph reached for the piano to steady himself. Looking into Steve's face he said, 'Yes sir, it's about time!'

"Oh, Lena, that *yes* must have soared to the courts of heaven. In my heart I heard the music of a thousand angels singing, 'Rejoice, rejoice for the Lord brings back His own.' "

Lena's black face, wet with tears, looked out the kitchen window. "I thanks You, Jesus. I done birthed my child in the Spirit. We carried him nine months and now he is birthed!"

There was a camp meeting in the kitchen. "Our child done come crying out to God, and now he come naked to be clothed in His righteousness. And soon we be seeing shoes on his feet and a ring on his finger. There be feasting in the land! Hallelujah!"

"Lena, that meeting didn't end until midnight. Then Steve said, 'I'm coming home with you, Ralph. We'll study the Word together and reach out to others like you. No more running away!'

"Well, Lena, guess who else was there? Billy Welker! You should have seen those two rascals rejoicing together. The rejoicing continued until 4 A.M. at home and I made cocoa and grilled cheese sandwiches and we finally went to bed. That's why I didn't call you, but I might have known the Lord would tell you.

"The last thing Ralph and Billy said to each other was that they were rounding up their old friends from Hamburger Hill and inviting them for supper, so Steve can talk to them and they can tell what happened to them. On my way to work this morning I asked the Lord—like you do, Lena—'I wonder how many there will be?' "

"I can tell you," Lena interrupted, because I got the knowing that you be having twenty-three young'uns."

"Lena! That's the number I got!"

"Why you so surprised?"

"That's not all, Lena. I said out loud in the car, 'I wonder what I can prepare?' "

"I can tell you that, too!"

"Oh, oh, Lena—don't tell me the Lord gave you a knowing menu!"

"Tell me what knowing you got, then I tell you my knowing."

"I got this menu—hamburgers, baked beans, applesauce, and pound cake—but Lena, I said to myself, *That's an easy menu—but no way I can bake a pound cake.* The strangest thing happened, Lena, I got a real knowing, *pound cake!*"

Lena's laughter filled the kitchen. "What you think I be toting in that bag? Look—here be the mixer, the sugar, the butter, and the pound-cake tin—everything we need for the pound cake. The Lord woke me up and said, 'Lena, you get your tote bag. Today you bake a pound cake in the infirmary. Sister Jensen be needing a big pound cake to go with hamburgers, baked beans, and applesauce.' "

"That old stove? The only thing that stove bakes is oven toast!" I laughed and cried at the same time.

Lena scrubbed out the stove and took authority over the coonching spirits that make a pound cake fall. There was no way to regulate the temperature correctly, but Lena prayed, sang, and mixed the cake. It turned out perfect!

"Lena, did I ever tell you how much I love you?"

"Oh, child—at least a hundred times! Now I ask you— why you so surprised when God tells Lena to bake a cake? Didn't Elijah tell that woman in the Bible to bake a cake? God don't change!"

With pound cake in my car I headed for home at the close of the day.

Before going home I had to stop at the store for applesauce. Standing in line I saw a beautiful girl whom I had met previously. Impulsively I called out, 'Come over for hamburgers. Having a gang of young people. And bring friends along! See you later.' Then I was off to get the grill out for Dan and put the beans in the oven.

They came in vans and motorcycles; barefooted, long-haired, and hungry. The warm September air made outdoor serving easy. The girls from school helped pour gallons of tea and Dan kept grilling hamburgers. Platters of baked beans, applesauce, and hamburgers made the rounds. The final touch was a piece of pound cake served on a napkin. When the count was complete, we had served twenty-three people. There was one hamburger left over. Jo Jo, the beagle, came around the corner and caught that one.

I watched the young people sitting on the lawn. Steve was talking earnestly. Later he prayed with three notorious drug pushers.

The prophetic word was being fulfilled, "A servant of the Lord will come to minister to Ralph. Great will be his deliverance and the deliverance of many." I had a knowing that this was only the beginning.

20

Shoes on His Feet

"Here comes my child with the preacher man! I best be putting on another pot of coffee."

Lena bustled in the kitchen, and when the door opened with a "Hallelujah! Praise the Lord, Sister Lena!" she was ready with a "Thank You, Jesus." Looking at Ralph, she laughed, "And who might that one be?"

With a bear hug she wrapped her arms around Ralph's lean frame and rested her head against him. "Oh, Lord Jesus done found our child and now he gets shoes on his feet to go with good news."

Steve and Lena were like twin volcanoes, ready to erupt with praises of joy. Then they settled into conversation.

"Ralph is going with me to the mountains of Virginia to give his testimony. Then I leave for Kentucky where my family is waiting. My work is finished here, but I'll be back."

Steve grew thoughtful. "Lena, we can't let up. You and I know the enemy is powerful, so pray for me, when you pray for the others."

"I just calls out the army of the Lord for you, preacher man, and God not be forgetting how you be obedient to Him."

When there was a break in my work I came out of the office to join the others for coffee.

"Lena, you should have seen Steve yesterday morning. He was pacing the floor and yelling for Ralph to get out of the bathroom—with that *beard off!*

"What a Sunday morning!"

Steve and Ralph were laughing, but Steve managed to continue. "Ralph had been asked to give his testimony in High Point, so Saturday I bought a ten dollar tie to go with his new clothes. 'Nothing but the best,' I told him. Oh, Lena, that beard. What a hassle! There's nothing wrong with a beard. I told Ralph, 'Grow ten beards later—but this beard is an identification with the old drug crowd, and now all things are new.'[1] It was the same hassle with Billy's hair. He jumped out of the barber's chair three times—said chains were pulling him away from obedience."

Ralph joined in, "Billy said the pull was so great that he had to hold onto the barber chair, and he yelled, 'Cut it fast!' The barber thought he was crazy. When he finished, Billy said he felt free, like the chains were off for good. That's how it was with me. Lena, I had to hold onto the piano Tuesday night. I actually felt a demonic power leave my body and I was floating and felt free at last. Few people can understand the power of Satan. It's a miracle I ever got away from my old friends."

"Oh, praise Jesus," Lena shouted. "I knows that the power in the blood be greater. Jesus just pushed that stone away so no one be locked in prison. Jesus sets us free.

"One night your mama be praying mighty hard and she cried out, 'Oh, Jesus, let Ralph come forth from that prison tomb of sin.' Then she be praising God, and thanking her Jesus for rolling the stone away. Then your mama got a song and called your Aunt Doris and she sang the song on the telephone. Pretty soon your Aunt Doris and your mama sang the song together and now we be calling that song the 'Family Victory Song'—for the whole family."

> We are triumphant people
> Marching on to Zion
> Marching to the city of our God
> We are more than conquerors in Him
> We are more than conquerors in Him
> To sing the praises of our Lord
> To sing the praises of our Lord
> We are triumphant people
> Marching on to Zion
> Marching to the city of our God.

Lena poured more coffee and passed the oven toast. "What I want to know, child, did you get to the meeting in time? What happened to your toe?"

Ralph laughed. "My poor toe, well, Steve prayed for it. After all, the prodigal had to have shoes on his feet. When I put the shoe on, the pain was gone."

"Glory to Jesus! The prodigal done got birthed like I said and come crying out to the Lord, naked, and he got new clothes, and now got shoes on his feet. Next thing, this child get a ring on his finger—and we been feasting right now on oven toast and jam."

Steve continued, "When that crowd saw Ralph walk in, with his face shining like glory, dressed in that sport coat and ten dollar tie, they burst into applause. Ralph just smiled and said, 'Oh, how I love Jesus.' There was nothing to add, Lena, he said it all."

"Now child, you got your feet shod with the gospel of peace. You be mighty careful where you walk. Stay out of that Satum's place. Don't be thinking you can walk in and convert that devil crowd. You just bring one by one to the Jesus crowd. There the power in the blood be greater. That

Satum sets traps for the birthed ones. I hates that Satum! Don't go near his traps. Stay away from the chains. You been set free—*now stay free!* That Mr. Mason at the prayer meeting keep saying, 'Keep yourselves, little children—keep yourselves in the love of Jesus. Keep yourselves in the Word of God. Keep yourselves close to other believers.'[2]

"Jesus washed you clean by His blood, and baptized you with the Holy Ghost and power so you be strong in the Lord and in the power of His Light. You puts on that whole "army" of God. He put joy in your soul, so now don't let those coonching spirits of the past come crowding out the joy. The Holy Spirit is given to those who obey. Now how He going to guide you if you don't obey? Jesus set you free so you can choose to obey. Now up to you to choose right. Praise the Lord!

"That be for you, too, preacher man. God be no respecter of persons. We all coming short of the glory of God. That Satum bring up the past cause he got no future. Only Jesus got the future and now is the day of salvation. One thing I do be knowing—God not forgetting that you be the servant of the Lord who obeyed His voice. God not the forgetting kind. You be mighty special to God, preacher man."

The kitchen grew quiet. We were on holy ground. Lena sang softly:

Without Him I would be nothing . . .

Softly she added, "Go tell them on the mountain—go with your feet shod with the gospel of peace. Go, in Jesus' name, and I'll be calling out your name."

21

Songs of the Heart

I stood by the open window of the infirmary kitchen, looking out over the sleeping campus. The morning was cool and dark, with shades of light coming through the towering oak branches outside the window. I was alone, with peace in my heart and stillness around me.

From deep within me came a prayer of thanksgiving and I found myself singing a song, with words and a melody I had never heard before.

> Who can tell a tree how to grow?
> Who can tell a seed how to sow?
> Who can tell a river how to flow?
> Who can tell the love that I know?
>
> CHORUS:
>
> For it's like a mighty river
> Coming from above
> It's like a mighty river from the heart of God
> It's like a mighty river, deep, deep as the sea
> It's a river of love for you and me.

Who can tell the sun how to shine?
Who can tell the world that it's mine?
Who can tell the stars what course to go?
Who can tell the love that I know?

So much had happened—young people coming and go-ing, not only to talk to Steve, but to see if Ralph had really been changed. Phone calls came from Massachusetts, chains attempting to pull him back. I served cocoa and grilled cheese sandwiches all hours of the night. I'd gotten little sleep, but I was at peace.

The quiet of the early morning enfolded me like a blan-ket, and once again I was singing a new song:

I just want to say thank You
Thank You, God above
I just want to say thank You
Thank You for Your love
I just want to thank Jesus
Praise His name all day
Thank You Holy Spirit
For showing Ralph the way.

I remembered the Scripture verse Ezekiel 34:11: "For thus saith the Lord God; Behold I, even I, will both search my sheep, and seek them out." The memory of a dark night of the soul came back to me when I had opened my Bible and read Ezekiel 34 over and over.

I found myself singing another new song:

My Jesus found him
And brought him back home.
My Jesus found him
When he wandered alone.
He picked him up on His shoulder
Out of the cold—cold—cold

And He brought him home
Safe in the fold.

CHORUS:

Oh, hallelujah, Oh, praise the Lord
Oh, hallelujah, Oh, praise the Lord
He picked him up on His shoulder
Out of the cold—cold—cold
And He brought him home
Safe in the fold.

I heard a step behind me and knew it was Lena. She joined in, and it seemed as though all the battles of the last nine months evaporated with the morning dew. We worshiped together.

With a "Praise the Lord," and a "Thank You, Jesus," Lena turned to the practical part of the day and reached for the coffeepot. "Best be getting some toast in the oven," Lena laughed. "We can sing while we work. So much coming and going in this infirmary we has to work twice as hard when we work. Lots of cleaning up to do and the laundry man coming. Here comes Zeb, the trash man.

"Good morning, Zeb. Been wondering how long you be singing in that church quartet?"

"Oh Lena, ah reckon, near 'bout fifty year now. Some songs folks be hearin' over and over."

"Nurse Jensen's son just got birthed in the Spirit, Zeb, and we be singing praises. We be mighty proud if you get a beat for us, Zeb."

Like a gnarled tree, bent with years of labor, Zeb sat down on the garbage can. His face looked like weathered tree bark, framed by white hair, like cotton. He tapped his worn shoe and got a beat, and with rolling sound he hummed. Words came between humming.

On Jordan's stormy banks I stand
Oh Lord, I been trabblin'
This lonesome road
I casts a wishful eye
Oh Lord, I be lookin' to Home
Oh who will come and go with me
This world be a lonesome road
Where my possessions lie
I be trabblin' mighty light, oh, Lord
I am bound for the Promised Land
Oh who will come and go with me
Don't want to trabble this lonesome road alone
I am bound for the Promised Land
Hummm Hummm—Cause we be trabblin' on
Thank You, Jesus, I'm coming Home.

I watched Zeb go across campus. He was still singing, "I be trabblin' on."

The day's work seemed to move ahead without effort. The routine sick calls, beds to make, excuse slips, medication, and order reports. It seemed that the campus was protected from harm or accidents. Students were happy and adjusting well. Word spread quickly among the Christian students that their prayers had been answered. Ralph was home—free! Others who didn't understand, somehow knew this was a miracle, and came to ask questions. For many it was a time of searching.

Steve and Ralph stopped by to share their plans, and discussed the many invitations Ralph was getting to share his testimony.

"Don't be forgetting that Satum got a big army of coonching spirits—but always be remembering that God has His big army of angels and ministering spirits. God's army is bigger. Just stay close to Jesus and put on the whole "army" of God."

We watched them leave. Lena was standing by the window—calling out their names—and getting a beat for a new song.

She grabbed the broom, and in her own way routed out the debbil's army of coonching spirits. With a swoosh of the broom, and a beat in her feet, she sang:

> Satum, your kingdom must come down
> Oh, Oh, Satum, your kingdom must come down
> You been building your kingdom all over this
>   land
> .   *But*—Swoosh— Swoosh
> Your kingdom coming down
>   Swoosh! Swoosh!

With a triumphant sweep of the broom she marched:

> Jesus, Your kingdom building up
> Jesus, Your kingdom building up

In the name of Jesus we had the victory. In the name of Jesus, Satum had to flee.

Another day had come to a close.

22

A Time for Joy

The leaves made a soft carpet on the trail beside the lake. Red and gold trees reflected in the water on which the geese and ducks swam. Against the blue sky, the lazy clouds drifted slowly apart to allow the sun to cast its golden splendor over the close of an October day.

We walked quietly, my sister Doris and I, for our thoughts were winging heavenward.

Days piled upon days with ceaseless joy and praise, like the ocean rolling its waves toward the shore. I had been in the valley of agony, and now with eagle's wings, I was on the mountain of praise. I didn't want to come down.

Tugging at the backroads of my mind was the devotional reading in *My Utmost for His Highest*[1] in which the author, Oswald Chambers says, "We are built for the valley—where we prove our mettle."

As though reading my mind, Doris reminded me of what Harold Bredesen said to me when I came bouncing into a meeting with the news of Ralph's conversion. "Remember, Margaret, prepare for the next battle. The warfare continues, and we win battle by battle."

"Oh, Do, I also remember when he told me that my joy didn't depend on my family being right with God, but my joy was Jesus."

Doris answered, "Remember when you begged Evelio Perez to talk to Ralph, and you were upset because Evelio said, 'Ralph is not ready yet—but he will come'? Our family is so used to making things happen that it is hard to learn to wait on the Lord."

"It seems God is allowing us to be shaken free of our preconceived notions, so that what is real cannot be shaken," Doris continued. "Nothing is as important as our relationship with Jesus Christ. I read about the three questions that come to us: 'Believe ye that I am able to do this?' 'Do I really know my risen Lord?' 'Do I know the power of His indwelling Spirit?' Faith should be as natural as breathing, so we don't stagger at God's promises."

"See that tree over there, Do? I remember last November, on a cold rainy day, when I put on my raincoat and went walking this trail alone. I was crying over Ralph so hard I could hardly walk. When I came to that old tree I just put my arms around that rough bark and wept my heart out. Then I beat my fists into the tree in frustration and cried out in anger, 'Oh, God, if any old beggar came to me like I'm begging you, I would grant any request within my power. I plead and beg for Ralph, but the heavens are brass. Why? Why? Your answer is silence.' In total despair I walked in the rain, with a dull aching inside. It was probably one of my darkest moments. Later, when I had sense enough to get dry and warm myself with a cup of hot tea, I read John 11:6. When Jesus heard that Lazarus was sick, Jesus waited two days before he went to visit him. I saw that God's silences are His answers.

"Later I learned to really pray believing—before the seeing. To think, Lena, with her childlike faith, was my teacher."

We followed the trail until we came to the stone bridge

over the Lake Euphemia. Sitting on the bridge we watched the water below.

"Ralph and Billy used to fish here when they were little boys."

It was quiet on the bridge, with the water running gently over the dam. Old friends, my sister and I, were comfortable with silence—or with rambling conversation.

"Margaret, do you remember that, years ago, we came to North Carolina at the same time—you to Greensboro, and my family to Winston-Salem? We didn't even know the other was coming. Since our family is scattered in other states, there must be a reason for us being here together."

"I guess it must have been for me, Do, or how would I have made it without the long walks and talks in these woods?

"Don't forget all those pots of coffee we drank—while talking a mile a minute. The best times we have is when we all get together. What a family we have! I want our children to enjoy each other like we do. Remember when someone said to you, 'Oh, I didn't know Margaret was your sister; I thought you were friends.' You answered, 'We are sisters—and best friends.' I like that!"

"Mother wrote that every morning she and Dad read the Bible together and pray for each one of us by name. They not only claimed their children to live for God, but all the seed to come. What a heritage we have!"

We walked quietly with our thoughts of home: our mother, father, brother Gordon, and sister Grace in New York. Jeanelle, the youngest, in Florida, and Joyce in Chicago. Phone calls told the good news—Ralph was home *free*. All the family rejoiced together.

"We've been through some hard places in our family, but one thing is sure: When someone sends an S.O.S., everyone zeroes in to pray." Doris was quiet, then added thoughtfully, "We can't let up. Through these months we have learned something about prayer and intercession. 'Out of the mouth of babes and sucklings Thou has ordained strength—and wisdom!'[2] Lena has poured forth wisdom and strength that had to come from God. Her tenacious 'believing come before seeing' has become marching orders. We know that His Word is forever settled in heaven, so when we pray in His will, and it is not His will that any perish, then we know He hears and we receive the answer by faith."

"Oh, Do, I'll never forget that January morning when Lena said, 'If God had wanted you to die for Ralph, He would have asked you. Now who you be to tell God He not do enough when He sent His Son to die for Ralph?' A light went on inside me, and I learned a new way of living. There is the sacrifice of praise—which is faith in action. I read in Psalm 149:6, 'Let the high praises of God be in their mouth, and a two-edged sword in their hands.' Like Lena would say, 'Put on the whole army of God.' "

Slowly we headed back over the familiar path—thinking about all our children. What would it take for all to really know Him—the way, the truth, and the life? We felt like the two on the Emmaus road when Jesus walked with them, and their hearts burned within them. His presence was real on our trail. We walked softly over the fallen leaves.

"We have a great family, but we must learn now—the greatest work of all—the ministry of faith and intercession. It seems that we all read Oswald Chambers, even quote from him in family letters, and today we need to remember the one we read, 'Prayer does not fit us for the greater works; it *is* the greater work. . . . Prayer is the working of the miracle of redemption in me which produces the miracle of redemption in others by the power of God. . . . Prayer is the battle.' "[3]

The evening shadows fell across the road as we headed for home and a cup of coffee. After all the activity in our household it was good to sit together in a quiet kitchen. We knew we were coming down from the mountain into the valley where we prove our mettle.

Doris broke the silence with, "If two agree, it shall be done, so before I leave for home, let's do what Lena does—call out our children's names. First we offer praise and thanksgiving and make our petitions known. We don't know what the future holds for our children or their mates and the children to come, but we know the One who holds the future. Rebellion comes in many forms, sometimes obvious, sometimes subtle. Let's covenant together that all our children and their children will know the miracle of God's redemptive love. Our children have a godly heritage, but each one has to make a personal choice. We can't make that happen, but God can through the power of intercession."

We read again, "Prayer is the working of the miracle of redemption in me which produces the miracle of redemption in others by the power of God."

Later, I watched my sister ease her car past the lake, heading for her home. Like Lena, I stood by the window, calling out her name.

23

Christine

It was Monday morning again, and Lena was rattling pots and pans in the kitchen. I could hear the coffeepot getting into the act, and smell the oven toast. After a busy morning it would be a welcome break to sit down to a Lena lunch.

"I recall hearing someone say that if you want to be young, stay with young people, but if you want to die young, keep up with them." We laughed together while Lena poured coffee and served her cottage cheese and pineapple and grilled cheese.

"Whoever said that didn't count on the joy of the Lord to be their strength,"[1] Lena added with a chuckle. "We can do without sleep when so much joy going on."

"You should have seen Steve Bezuidenhaut, Lena! All weekend he was enjoying the young people, answering questions, or praying with someone. No one wants to go home these days, and the young people just come, sit on the floor, sing choruses, and share their experiences.

"There were some beautiful young people from Guilford College. Billy Welker was having a great time talking to all those lovely girls. Steve gave Ralph a nudge and said, 'Hey, good buddy, if I were a young man, and not married to my beautiful Wendy, I'd marry that girl."

"Ralph answered, 'I've been thinking about it, but I ought to get introduced first.'

"Those two are impossible!

"There were several beautiful girls, Lynn Marshall, Erras Davis, Georgianne Higgins, a darling redhead, Jane Craven, also Pat and Harold Small, newlyweds; and then there was Christine Fisher."

"That Ralph boy do have an eye for beautiful girls. Now which one he be looking at?"

"Believe it or not, Lena, I saw this girl at a meeting and I thought she had that Grace Kelly look, so poised and dignified, and there was also a warm friendliness about her. I fell in love with her myself and when I saw her at the grocery store, I called out to her to come over to the house, and bring her friends.

"She was so friendly and said she'd probably come with her roommate, Jane Craven. There were a lot of young people at the house, but I couldn't help but notice that lovely, tall blond girl—Christine Fisher. She's a senior at Guilford College, and her hometown is Elizabeth City."

"Wait a minute, child, does she know Jesus? That Ralph boy needs time to grow up in the Lord."

"Oh, Lena, they just met. I do know this, that she was invited to a Campus Crusade retreat and there she learned that Jesus loved her and had a plan for her life. She accepted Jesus as her Savior, and I heard her say that she knew that God would lead her step by step. She has a beautiful quiet trust in God.

"I am amazed at the spiritual insight these new Christians have. That's not all, Lena, these beautiful young people went to Hyannis, Massachusetts, to witness under Campus Crusade. That's the secret, get into Bible study, learn to pray, and then go out and share your faith. Well, Lena, looks like we see so many young people who live for the things of the world that we forget how many wonderful Christians there are on the school campuses. I can't wait for you to meet all these lovely girls.

"Uncle Howard is visiting from Chicago, and when he saw Christine Fisher, he said to Ralph, 'Now, Ralph, if I were a young man—that's the girl I'd marry.'

"Then Ralph says, 'Uncle Howie, I'm thinking about it!' "

Lena was about to have church in the kitchen. "Thank You, Jesus! You never fail! You said for that child to rise up and walk and everything he longed for would be where he left it—right back at his father's house.

"Now, don't you go organizing just cause you love that girl!" Lena laughed while she shook her finger at me. "You best leave it to Jesus. That Ralph be getting himself in more trouble; now this time the Lord be showing my child the right way. Jesus first, then all the good things follow. If God make the world in six days, and give Eve to Adam, well, I guess He can make a new Ralph and give him the girl he always dreamed of. God sure can get a lot done in six days."

The days ran together like a river of joy. One night Ralph came home. "Mama and Daddy, I have something to tell you!"

"Chris and I drove out to the airport and I was thinking of how I had always longed for a girl like Chris—so much like Jan in so many ways. Then I also realized I had nothing to offer, and how could I ever expect to deserve a girl like Chris. Before I realized it, I was saying out loud all the thoughts of my heart. It was as though the things I couldn't say, the Holy Spirit was saying for me. For the first time in my life, I knew what real love was. She had everything I longed for—a beautiful Christian girl, and so easy to talk to. Mom and Dad, it just had to be the Lord, because that beautiful girl said she would marry me. Just like you said, Mom, everything I longed for, right back at father's house. I still can't believe it! All these years. I'm running away from God, and He just waited for me to turn around."

Harold was shouting, "Praise the Lord, Ralph! 'He is able to do abundantly above all we can ask or think.' Now, young man, you and I are going right out to pick out a ring for that girl God gave to you."

I couldn't wait to tell Lena, and when we got together we had church in the kitchen.

"Look at that Mr. Jensen, so happy, you'd think he be the one getting married, and Dan boy, too. He's remembering how he sat in the chair and prayed for his brother. There's joy in the camp today."

Lena got her beat, and while the coffeepot perked she clapped her hands and started singing:

> I've got peace like a river in my soul.

"Lena, Chris just fits into the family like she was born into it. Jan will love her like a sister. You won't believe what we all did last night, but then by now you can believe anything." Lena laughed. I continued. "Ralph took Chris into the other room, and when they came out, they had been crying for joy. Chris just held up that finger with a diamond ring on it. She was so happy. Harold said, 'O.K., now we'll go out to eat and go to the State Fair in Raleigh.' I got so excited I wanted them to pick out their china at Belks. You never saw such a family—everyone wanting to do something.

"Chris and Ralph walked all over the fair. What a way to celebrate! Every once in a while she'd hold up that hand and show the ring."

Looking out the window, Lena saw them coming up the driveway. "They even look alike," Lena laughed.

Within a few minutes Ralph was saying, "Lena, meet the girl God gave me, Christine Fisher."

24

The Master's Touch

The following days were filled with joyous expectation—except for one problem: Ralph needed permanent work. He could always find temporary jobs, but he was searching for work with a purpose.

"The Lord not bring that boy home to leave him flitting around with no roots. God promised work, so he get work." Lena was talking to herself in the kitchen, and that was my signal to stop for my coffee break.

"God never goes halfway. You wrote in that letter to our boy, and God will do what He said—and that be a work, not just a job, but a work God will give him. There be jobs, and then there be a work. The jobs come along to give that piece of money to pay the rent. Sometimes that be a waiting time until God says, 'Now I give you a work to do.' That be a knowing that your work is unto the Lord, even if it be on the job. Some folks never learn that the cooking, cleaning, sweeping, and yard work, mopping and carrying out garbage cans, is a work, an offering to God—well pleasing in His sight.

"Now we stand still and see. Can't see, running. While Ralph talking to all the bossmen about a job, we best be stretching out before the Lord. The Word says to knock and the right door will open. You just keep knocking till the knowing comes. You keep seeking; can't stop till you find. Nothing in this world be easy. You keep asking until the answer comes.[1] That Satum—oh how I hates that Satum—he come slinking around to close doors God be opening, and to make you stop before the finding. He just come slipping around to kill, steal, or to destroy. That Satum so mad he got beat out of this child he try most anything. We know one thing—Jesus in our child be greater. Hallelujah! We just calls out the army of the Lord, that's what we do. Every good and perfect gift comes from above. All the bad come from that Satum.

"Out, Satum, out!" Lena grabbed the broom with a fury. "Satum, your kingdom must come down! I know your tricks! Jesus defeated you on the cross. That's why you hate the cross so much. Jesus just moved into Ralph boy and no way you win over Jesus. Jesus saved him from your hell—that's what my Jesus did. You lost your power. Out Satum!!! Out!!!

"No use talking soft-like to that rascal! The Bible says resist, and I reckon resist means what it say—you push harder than he do, and you cry out louder than that debbil can roar. In the name of Jesus our child will do the work God has for him. God never promises halfway. Time we be learning not to give up until the victory all won! Too many folks falling by the wayside. Too many turning around, Sister Jensen. Too many not following all the way. I feels a beat coming in my feet, and a tune coming in my head, and the words coming from the heart. MMMMM—O Lord—MMMMM—O Lord—HUMMMMM—O Lord—it's coming—"

> So many falling by the wayside
> O Lord help me to stand
> So many turning around Lord
> Please help me to stand
> Oh, my Jesus—help me to stand

I'm standing on Your Word, Lord
Help me to stand
I'm standing in Your name, Lord
Help me to stand
Oh, my Jesus, help me to stand.

The duties of the day demanded our attention, and the hours passed quickly. Before we realized it, it was time to head homeward. I heard Lena singing as she crossed the campus to the bus—"So many falling by the wayside. Help me to stand."

I knew she was going home to stretch out before the Lord. It was Tuesday, and tonight I would attend the Masons' prayer meeting.

When I arrived the place was filled, and the music was pouring forth the sound of joy. This time Ralph and Dan were a part of it. Later I eased over to my friend, Frances Dalton, and spoke with her about work for Ralph.

"What do you think he'd like to do?" she asked.

"Since his conversion, Frances, there is such a transformation that even his desires have changed. He says he wants to learn woodworking from the ground floor up. Now really, Frances, I never thought he could hammer a nail. Doesn't seem the type. His teachers predicted he'd be a lawyer. He says that he feels a call to woodworking, just like a call to medicine or the ministry. No one in our family is known for craftsmanship."

"We'll just pray together, Margaret, and I'll talk to Hunter, Junior. God will open the right door."

And so it came to pass that Ralph went to work for the Snow Lumber Company in High Point. The owner was Hunter Dalton, Jr.

I learned later that Hunter didn't receive the suggestion with too much enthusiasm, but Mama had persuasive powers

Hunter could not resist. He never regretted that decision, for Ralph learned well—from the bottom up!

One day while holding a piece of rough wood in his hand, he remembered a poem his beloved Bestemör (grandmother) used to give at family gatherings:

The Touch of the Master's Hand

'Twas battered and scarred, and the auctioneer
Thought it scarcely worth his while
To waste much time on the old violin,
But held it up with a smile.
"What am I bidden, good folks," he cried,
"Who will start bidding for me?
"A dollar, a dollar, a dollar"—then, "Two!" Only two?
"Two dollars and who'll make it three?
"Three dollars once; three dollars twice;
"Going for three—" But no,
From the room, far back, a gray-haired man
Came forward and picked up the bow;
Then, wiping the dust from the old violin,
And tightening the loose strings,
He played a melody pure and sweet,
As sweet as a caroling angel sings.

The music ceased, and the auctioneer,
With a voice that was quiet and low,
Said, "What am I bidden for the old violin?"
And he held it up with the bow.
"A thousand dollars, and who'll make it two?
"Two thousand! And who'll make it three?
"Three thousand once; three thousand twice;
"And going, and gone!" said he.
The people cheered, but some of them cried,
"We do not quite understand

"What changed its worth?" Swift came the reply:
"The touch of the master's hand."

And many a man with life out of tune,
And battered and scattered with sin,
Is auctioned cheap to the thoughtless crowd,
Much like the old violin.
A "mess of pottage," a glass of wine;
A game—and he travels on.
He's "going" once, and "going" twice,
He's "going" and "almost gone."
But the Master comes, and the foolish crowd
Never can quite understand
The worth of a soul, and the change that's wrought
By the touch of the Master's hand.[2]
—Myra Brooks Welch

Ralph had a knowing in his heart that the same creative, redemptive power of God that changed his life would also release the creative power within him to bring beauty out of a piece of rough wood. This gift from God was within him and like the Bible said, he would stir up that gift within him by hard work and study, and learning God's principles for successful living.

Lena's answer to all the blessings was that God never goes halfway. "God gave Ralph his work unto the Lord—while on the job in the lumberyard."

Later, much later, Ralph named his own furniture manufacturing company, "The Master's Touch." His beautiful eighteenth century reproductions stand in spacious homes as a silent witness to the creative, redemptive power of God. When people ask about the name at furniture showings, he quietly tells the story of the Master's touch.

One day Ralph told of his attempt to hide his stained hands

while sitting in church. The presence of the Lord drew near during that worship service and he had a knowing in his heart, "Your hands are beautiful to Me." With a heart of thanksgiving he raised his heart and hands in praise and worship.

Upon hearing that incident, I sat down, and for his birthday I wrote the following poem:

Hands

His hand was soft upon my breast,
Tiny fingers curled in sleep.
I offered to God, and him, my best,
A promise, within our love to keep.

His hands grew firm and strong
To hold a bat, or pitch a ball.
Oh, God, keep him from wrong;
Let him grow good, as well as tall.

Then one day he walked away
And waved his hand farewell.
I wept tears like ocean spray.
How far, oh, God, who can tell?

Then one day the Master came—
"Come, take My hand, My son.
For you alone, My life I gave
That we could be as one."

There stands my son, the Master's touch
Upon his heart and hands;
God so loved, He gave so much.
Now, in His power he stands.

The Master Carpenter of Galilee
Made a table out of wood,
Shaped it from His created tree,
Took it from His forest, where it stood.

He took man, made by God
And melted his heart of stone;
This bit of clay, from earth's sod,
He chose to be His own.

Within my son's firm hand
He holds a rough-hewn tree,
And carves an altar to stand
A gift—in God's sanctuary.

He lifts his heart and hands in praise,
His God of all creation,
In song of triumph, hallelujahs raise—
How great is Thy salvation!

When Craig Hyman, a Greensboro artist, read the poem
and heard the story, he drew Ralph's hands. The poem, in
Craig's script writing, and his lifelike drawing now hang in our
guest room which is furnished with Ralph's creative master-
pieces.

25

The Wedding

Lena's face, a symphony of joy, looked up at Dan. Her big black eyes were filled with wordless wonder. Dressed in simple elegance, with a soft stole around her shoulders, she walked down the aisle like a queen at her coronation. With dignity she was ushered to the pew of the stately Trinity Methodist Church, Greensboro, North Carolina.

The music filled the sanctuary as Margaret Weymann blended her melodious harp with her mother's organ playing. Cy and Chris Moffit, leaders of Christine's Bible study, joined their voices in beautiful songs of love and joy.

Red poinsettias blended with palms in the glow of soft candlelight. "Joy to the World" and "Oh Holy Night" seemed to describe the occasion. A Christmas wedding had all the sounds of angels' songs.

Lena sat quietly. This was her moment on the mountain to view the valley of the past and look ahead to a new beginning. From a side room I watched the guests stream into the church. How handsome the ushers looked in their tuxedos. I knew Lena was remembering the long hair and bare feet. The guests had not only come to attend a wedding, but to witness a miracle. It was a celebration of love, the love of God revealed in a manger and in the lives of new creations. It was not only a time to rejoice in the love of two young people; but to be a part of the love of an entire family and friends who had wept and prayed together. For unto all of us the Savior indeed had come. Somehow I knew the angels were singing again, "Glory to God in the highest." I knew I was.

Lena, humble servant of the Lord, sat with a knowing in her heart. Her face reflected that steadfast walk of faith. I called out to her silently, in my heart, "Well done, thou good and faithful servant."

The people kept coming! There was Skipper Bowles, a prominent political figure, sitting quietly with tears in his eyes. As a friend, he, too, had tried to help Ralph. Dr. James Bruce, beloved friend and physician, came with a believing heart, for he had seen the miracle.

The white-haired patriarch, Mr. James Mason, and his musical family, the Talleys, sat together. Bob Adams and his golden clarinet would join the musicians later at the reception. Our dear friend, Frances Dalton, came with Hunter. In my heart I was saying, *Beautiful lady, I love you, and I thank you, Hunter, for giving Ralph work.* They were part of the miracle. Somehow I knew Lena was shouting on the inside when she watched the prayer meeting crowd come in. Ralph and Chris Kyle had come from Atlanta to see the new Ralph and meet the new Chris. The young and old blended together; some in blue jeans, others in diamonds and furs. Tonight we were one!

Joy and thanksgiving welled up within when I watched my family being ushered to their pews. My sisters, Grace, Doris, Joyce, and Jeanelle had wept with me in the valley; now they rejoiced with me on this holy night. My brother, Gordon, and his family came from New York City to be a part of the celebration. Those handsome nieces and nephews! How I loved them all! Harold's brothers, Jack and Howard, and his sisters, Harriette and Fern, were all united in love. Although some of our extended family could not be present, I sensed their rejoicing with us. The touch of the Master's hand reached out to all the family.

Then came our own Janice and Jud Carlberg—faithful children—and now parents themselves. As the first-born from each family, they set a beautiful example for all the others to follow. Now Jan would have a sister, Chris. Dan and Ralph had another brother in Jud. "Oh, God, send the right girl for Dan," I prayed quietly.

"Come, Queen Elizabeth," Dan smiled into Bestemör's beaming face. She patted his hand with a "Thank you, dear," and proudly walked the aisle.

"Mom, it's now your turn." With my arm in Dan's we walked together with Harold following. I wanted to shout to all my family and friends, "O magnify the Lord with me and let us exalt His name together—for this our son who was dead is alive. Thank you for coming to the wedding feast." I just quietly smiled to everyone and let my praise be unto the Lord. My cup was full and running over.

Although it was difficult for Christine's family to understand the miraculous power of God, they rejoiced with us. Her lovely sisters and their families were now a part of our family. Chris's mother, Frances, looked elegant in blue. Events had moved too quickly for her understanding, but she would someday realize that God's ways are not always our ways. We would be good friends, I knew in my heart.

The organ and the harp sounded out the wedding march.

The Reverend Roy Putnam stood quietly looking out over the full sanctuary.

Dan and Ralph waited. How handsome they looked. Ralph turned to smile at me. He was reading my thoughts. The beautiful girls in green velvet dresses walked slowly down the aisle. Jane's red hair was shining in the candlelight. *How could that handsome Billy ever have been such a rascal?* I thought to myself. Then the organ poured forth the majestic chords that brought everyone to their feet.

Ralph's face wore an expression of awe and wonder while he watched God's precious gift walking toward him.

Christine Fisher, in white velvet winter wonderland, came down the aisle on the arm of her father, "Bo Bo" Fisher, retired Coast Guard Commander, who reluctantly relinquished his youngest daughter.

Before the wedding I had whispered to him, "Someday, Bo Bo, you will understand God's miracle of grace." He stood proud and handsome.

Chris looked like a Christmas angel: her face a picture of transparent joy. Facing each other, Ralph and Chris spoke their vows. They seemed to be enwrapped in the sight and sound of Christmas love and joy. They knelt together while the heavens watched. The unseen Guest seemed to whisper, "I love you all with an everlasting love. Continue in My love for each other."

The beautiful service ended. Pastor Putnam pronounced Ralph and Chris man and wife—in the presence of God and in this assembly.

The music burst forth in joyous celebration, "A mighty fortress is our God, a bulwark never failing."

During the reception Lena held court. Everyone wanted to meet her. When friends asked, "How long have you known Ralph?" she answered: "All my life. All my life. I birthed him."

I managed to sit beside her for a moment. "How did you keep from shouting, Lena?"

"Same way you did," she laughed. "I just shouted on the inside, but now I can say, 'Hallelujah, praise the Lord, and thank You, Jesus!' Now tell me, where they be going?"

"Lena, you won't believe what these cousins and friends have been up to. They think Ralph and Chris are going to Morehead and those rascals have a car ready to follow loaded with fishing gear. Well, Harold reserved the honeymoon suite at the Holiday Inn at Wrightsville Beach. Uncle Ralph is going to drive them in his car to their hidden car. They are changing their clothes now and everyone is getting ready to throw rice. Lena, just think, all my family will be together for Christmas."

Under a shower of rice we watched the newlyweds as they were whisked away to their honeymoon at the North Carolina beach. "What God hath joined together. Let no man put asunder."

Lena waved until they were out of sight, then raised her eyes to heaven. She was calling out their names.

Epilogue

It is 1996!

I reached for the phone and dialed Greensboro, North Carolina.

"Lena, I just had to wish you a happy new year and tell you we all returned from Heather's wedding in Massachusetts. She is the baby you prayed for.

"That's not all! Ralph and Chris are on a second honeymoon to celebrate their twenty-fifth wedding anniversary. Remember December 19, 1970?

"Ralph has his own furniture business, The Master's Touch, and is an elder in the Presbyterian church. Chris teaches in a Christian school. Shawn, the child of promise, is 23; Eric is 21; Sarah 17; and Kathryn, 14.

"My 'hippie boys'—now serving the Lord—have children attending Gordon College."

"Praise the Lord! Thank You, Jesus!" Lena shouted. "God brought us all through some stormy years, but He never failed.

"Your Harold gone Home, and my Mr. Leach, 93 years old, went Home to be with Jesus."

"Are you living alone, Lena?"

"No, child. Jesus lives right here, and we get along fine. The same Dr. Gilmore who took care of the younguns at school now takes care of me—God bless him!"

"Remember how we used to sing 'we walk by faith, not by sight—just take one step at the time?' "

"I remember! Come soon and we'll get a beat and sing again."

"I'll bring Chad, Jan's son, the one you prayed for when he was a baby."

"Lord have mercy! That child growed up!"

"Lena, I am thankful that God spared you during the long illness after heart surgery. We love you and need you."

"Take our hand, precious Lord, lead us on in this new year."

"Praise the Lord!"

Notes

Chapter 1
1. Proverbs 3:6

Chapter 2
1. Psalm 1
2. Psalm 19
3. John 14:6
4. Proverbs 3:6

Chapter 3
1. Isaiah 40:1
2. Psalm 19
3. Charles H. Spurgeon, *Treasury of David*, 2d ed. (New York: Funk & Wagnalls, 1882), p. 305.

Chapter 9
1. Isaiah 40:31

Chapter 10
1. 2 Chronicles 20:3,15,17
2. Jude 21 and Hebrews 12:2

Chapter 11
1. Charles H. Spurgeon, *Treasury of David*, 2d ed. (New York: Funk & Wagnalls, 1882), p. 88.

Chapter 12
1. Matthew 16:26
2. Proverbs 14:12
3. John 14:6
4. John 15:12
5. Luke 6:38

Chapter 13
1. Luke 15

Chapter 17
1. 2 Corinthians 6:2
2. Philippians 3:13

Chapter 19
  1. John 3:3

Chapter 20
  1. 2 Corinthians 5:17
  2. Jude 21

Chapter 22
  1. Oswald Chambers, *My Utmost for His Highest* (New York: Dodd, Mead & Co., 1935), p. 275.
  2. Psalm 8:2
  3. Chambers, *My Utmost*, p. 291

Chapter 23
  1. Nehemiah 8:10

Chapter 24
  1. Matthew 7:7
  2. From *Best Loved Poems of the American People*, published in 1936.

Other Good
Harvest House Reading

FIRST WE HAVE COFFEE
by *Margaret Jensen*

Margaret's warm stories of life as the daughter of a Scandinavian pastor in the Canadian north will touch your heart with timeless lessons of unwavering faith and family love. Margaret's mother is an indomitable character whose stern Norwegian discipline is matched only by her laughter and singing. The down-to-earth wisdom she passes on to both young and old over steaming cups of coffee will bring encouragement and hope to anyone who has gone through difficult times.

ALL GOD'S CHILDREN GOT ROBES
by *Margaret Jensen*

Filled with poignant and often humorous stories, Jensen relates her personal experience with cancer to powerfully illustrate God's faithfulness and provision. With her special gift of sharing and warm sense of humor, *All God's Children Got Robes* will capture your heart and encourage you in your faith.

MEETING GOD IN QUIET PLACES
by *F. LaGard Smith*

Imagine yourself whisked away to the beautiful English countryside—walking down quiet lanes beside rambling dry-stone walls with spring flowers and summer grasses that reach out to touch you. In these inspiring parables drawn from daily walks, noted author Smith shares life-renewing insights to guide you to the very heart of God. When the daily clamor threatens to overwhelm you, these personal meditations will refresh both the eye and the soul, bringing renewed perspective to the values and qualities of life you cherish.

I STOLE GOD FROM GOODY TWO-SHOES
by *Heather Harpham*
This heartwarming collection of stories will tickle your funny bone
while showing God's surprisingly personal involvement in our
everyday lives. Filled with delightful, humorous "snapshots" of daily
living, Harpham captures the moment and focuses on what makes
ordinary occurrences extraordinary.